The World of the Crusaders

endpapers a reconstruction of Crusader propaganda in Europe: sections of a stained-glass window in the Monastery of St Denys. The glass was destroyed during the French Revolution, but a drawing was preserved by an 18th-century French scholar

The World of the
CRUSADERS

Joshua Prawer

QUADRANGLE BOOKS
A New York Times Company

Published in the United States by Quadrangle Books, Inc.
330 Madison Avenue, New York, N. Y. 10017

Designed by Alex Berlyne for Weidenfeld and Nicolson

Library of Congress Catalog Card Number: 72–83624

ISBN 0 297 99537 5

Illustrations printed by Japhet Press, Tel Aviv;
text printed and book bound by Keter Press Ltd., Jerusalem

Contents

I

Three Empires and Four Claims

And God said unto Jacob, I am God Almighty: be fruitful and multiply; a nation and a company of nations shall be of thee, and kings shall come out of thy loins. And the land whic h I gave to Abraham and Isaac, to thee I will give it, and to thy seed after thee will I give the land (Genesis 35, 1–12).

For three millennia the destinies of lands, nations, religions and empires were determined by the Great Promise recorded in the Holy Scriptures. Countless millions were influenced by the words of Providence spoken to Jacob, son of Isaac, son of Abraham, the patriarchs of Israel. The concept of the Promised Land became a major tenet of the religion and hope of ancient Israel. It was destined to become an integral part of the heritage of all cultures which accepted the Holy Scriptures of Judaism or found affinity with the religion of Israel.

Christianity, which saw the fulfilment of the prophecies of salvation and deliverance in the advent of Jesus the Messiah, carried the Holy Scriptures and its own record of the Revelation throughout the Mediterranean and into the heart of the pagan empire, the city of Rome. The empire fell, but the new religion had already conquered it from within – a victory far more permanent than any of the ephemeral conquests of the barbarian chiefs who knocked at the doors of the capital – and Christianity spread to the tribes which bivouaced on the ruins of the great empire.

Christianity was more than a religion. It was a culture and a civilisation in which Athens and Rome blended with Jerusalem. The faithful inherited not only a cosmogony and the story of God who became Man to save humanity. His was the legacy of an elect nation, its vicissitudes and prophets, the greatest teachers of the most sublime ethics of mankind. With the story of the Hebrews – the Chosen People who had forfeited their privilege by rejecting the Saviour – the Christian was taught to view himself as heir to their claims and privileges. The New Testament issued from the Old Testament; the majestic personalities of the Old prefigured those of the New. Old Testament precepts dating back to the time when mankind lived under the Law were now obsolete and abolished.

The historical narrative of the Bible, with its tangible geographical setting, was metamorphosed and sublimated into the realm of the spiritual. Jerusalem, capital of the ancient kingdom, became Heavenly Jerusalem; and the kingdom of David became the realm of messianic times to come. Yet Bethlehem and Nazareth remained the places of the Annunciation and Nativity, and Jerusalem itself – with the Via Dolorosa, the Mount of Olives, Gethsemane, Golgotha and the Tomb of Christ – was more than just a point on a map of God's immense, flat world. Thus the Holy Land and the sites of Jesus's miracles and Passion became strangely real in the Christian consciousness. There was hardly a peasant in Christendom to whom the names of distant Judea and Galilee were unknown.

The teachings of the Church were common to all Christendom. But whereas there was no power in the semi-barbarian kingdoms of the West that could translate the Christian claim to the Holy Land into political terms, the situation was different in the Christian Orient, where Byzantium perpetuated the glory of Rome as well as the majesty of a Christian empire. In the beginning of the seventh century, the al-Rum, as it was called by its Moslem neighbours, stemmed a great Persian invasion and recovered the Holy Cross from Sassanide captivity. But no more than a generation later (ca AD 650), the swift horsemen of Arabia wrested from the empire the entire southern Mediterranean seaboard, including the African provinces and the shores of Palestine and Syria. At one time it seemed that even Constantinople would disappear in the waves of the Moslem flood. But Byzantium survived, and Constantinople continued to rule the Balkans and Asia Minor.

As head of a Christian empire and the guardian of Christian orthodoxy, the emperor of Byzantium was responsible for the defence and expansion of Christendom. This role was inherent in his title and was part of his legacy as successor to the first Christian emperor, Constantine the Great, and the rescuer of the Holy Cross, Emperor Heraclius. In the

opposite Alexius I Comnenus, emperor of Byzantium

tenth century the emperors Phocas and John I Zimisces (in 964–5 and 974–5, respectively) launched military expeditions against Islam in Asia Minor, Syria and Palestine that almost reached the very gates of Jerusalem. Emperor Phocas warned the caliph of Baghdad:

You living in the sands of the deserts, beware! Return to Sana [in Yemen]. Soon will I conquer Egypt and her riches will be my spoils . . . I will move against Mecca leading masses of warriors like the darkness of the night. I will capture this city to erect there the throne of God. Then will I turn to Jerusalem, will conquer East and West and everywhere will I erect the symbol symbol of the Cross.

The successors to the conquering Byzantine emperors claimed Syria and Palestine both on the strength of history and by right of religion. But when military strength failed to settle the issue, Byzantium's claim to the Holy Land was adapted to fit existing political and religious conditions, and the emperor of the East became the official protector of the Christian populations in lands under Moslem dominion. In reality, however, his role was confined to protection of the Byzantine Church, a *modus vivendi* accepted by the Moslem rulers. Nonetheless, while pragmatism prevailed in the interests of political expediency, the Byzantine emperor's claim to the Holy Land lasted the life of the empire and was raised against Moslem and crusader alike.

In the meantime, Western Christendom was creating its own social and political frameworks. New political entities slowly emerged from the whirlpool of the Germanic invasions of Western Europe. The legacy of Rome, insofar as it was preserved, became a part of the Church, where the splendours of the classical world found their last refuge. But there was no successor to Imperial Rome until Charles the Great (AD 800), who united the great expanses of Gaul, Germany and Italy under his rule. His military thrusts into heathen Saxony, Bohemia and Pannonia and his wars against Moslem Spain not only physically recreated the empire of the West, they were wars against the Infidel. His expeditions against the pagans, Moslems, Northmen, Slavs and Avars not only extended the boundaries of his political dominions, but also expanded the borders of Christendom and proliferated the True Faith. Consciousness of this aspect of the great emperor's campaigns endured for centuries. The *Chanson de Roland*, which at least had some historical basis, as well as the eleventh-century entirely legendary *Voyage de Charlemagne* (to the East) remained popular testimonies of the great emperor's confrontation with the Moslem Infidel. Three hundred years later, when Europe was on the march to engage Islam in Syria and Palestine, the majestic figure of Emperor Charlemagne still towered in European consciousness as the precursor of the Holy War.

The task of the lay head of Christendom, though never officially formulated, was to defend the security of the House of God and extend the boundaries of Christendom. Thus the claim to defend Christendom, which ultimately resulted in the call for a crusade, was made by both Christian Empires: Byzantium and the Holy Roman Empire in the West. At the end of the eleventh century, however, in the turmoil of the Investiture Contest – when papacy and empire were fighting for hegemony – the papacy took the lead, arrogating the prerogatives and obligations of empire. Indeed, it was the papacy of Hildebrand, the great Gregory VII, which launched the first appeal to fight the Infidel – and this a full generation before the First Crusade.

This papal appeal was contemporaneous with other movements stirring Western Europe. Two generations before Gregory VII, the daring marines of Genoa and Pisa set sail to fight the Infidel entrenched in the islands of the Mediterranean. Corsica and Sardinia, those nearest their home base, had been taken by the Moslems in the eighth century. Now the young Italian navies, which had served their apprenticeship plying the coasts of Provence and Spain, attacked the insular harbours both as bases of piracy and centres of power. The two islands became Christian, and Christendom acquired its first maritime bases outside the mainland. By the middle of the eleventh century (1064), French chivalry lent a hand to the fight against the Moslems in the Iberian Peninsula. Catalans and Provencals thrust southwards, marking their progress by the capture of Toledo in 1085. Soon the Spaniards from the small Christian principalities in the Pyrenees, Navarra, Aragon and Castile were foraging south, steadily driving back Islam from the northern parts of the peninsula. A later age called this movement a *reconquista*, the recovery of territories lost almost four hundred years before, when the Christian Visigothic kingdom was crushed by invading Moslems. Thus across the Mediterranean from Spain in the West, Sardinia and Corsica, soon to be followed by Malta in the centre, Western Christendom was fighting Islam to recover lost territories. In the context of this historical perspective, the Crusades to the Holy

Land represented the Eastern extension of the Christian Reconquista.

At the time of the First Crusade, the claims of Christendom – whether represented by pope or emperor, East or West – were balanced by the counter-claim and actual rule of Islam. Less than fifteen years after the flight of Mohammed from Mecca to Medina (AD 622), the prophet's warriors had penetrated from Arabia into Palestine, Syria and Asia Minor in the north and Egypt and northern Africa in the west. In the first great thrust to the north, Palestine and Syria fell to the Arabian horsemen, and Damascus became the capital of the Omayyad dynasty (661–650). Islam, which regarded itself as the latest Divine Revelation, inherited from Judaism and Christianity alike, and this saved the Holy Places of Palestine from utter destruction. Christians and Jews, as 'People of the Book' (*ahl al-kitab*) – and thus distinguished from pagans and Zoroastrians – became clients of the Moslem state – tolerated *dhimmi*, in the legal vocabulary of Islam. A legend had it that Omar, to whom the Byzantine patriarch of Jerusalem capitulated, did not perform his prayers in the Holy Sepulchre in a conscious effort to avoid creating a precedent which might later harm the Christians. His place of prayer became a mosque near the Holy Sepulchre (the Omariyah), but the Moslem conqueror was not satisfied with leaving it at that. The Koran tells of how Mohammed, after a miraculous night voyage, arrived on his fabulous mount Buraq at the Masjid al-Aqsa, the 'outer sanctuary', thus conferring sanctity on the city. When he arrived in Jerusalem, Omar asked to be shown the site of the Temple of the great King Suleiman (Solomon) and was dismayed to find that the area of the once-magnificent Jewish Temple was now no more than the city dump – Byzantium's monument to the victory of Christianity over Judaism. He immediately ordered that the area be cleared, and the first mosque in Jerusalem, al-Aqsa, a modest, temporary building of timber, was constructed. One hundred and fifty years later, in the centre of the holy area, Abd al-Malik erected the Haram ash-Sherif (691), the beautiful Dome of the Rock, which faced the Mosque of al-Aqsa at the edge of the esplanade.

For some two hundred years after the Moslem conquest, Jerusalem played only a minor role in the religious perspective of Islam. The *haj*, a pilgrimage incumbent upon every Moslem, was directed to the holy cities of Hejaz: Mecca and Medina. But Jerusalem's prestige was rising. In the eighth century, when political difficulties made access to Mecca difficult, the local pilgrimage to Jerusalem (the *zayara*) was declared a *haj* and thus attained a status equal to the pilgrimage to the holy cities of Hejaz. The caliphs and their local representatives went to great lengths to transform Byzantine Jerusalem into a Moslem centre. Tolerance towards non-Moslems began to deteriorate under Harun al-Rashid, the caliph of Baghdad (786–809), and official policy thereafter fluctuated between tolerance and pressure to convert. Decrees imposing on all non-Moslems distinctive dress and degrading signs – like large wooden crosses for Christians and bells for Jews – ultimately culminated in orders to destroy churches and synagogues. The caliph al-Hakim, the half-mad Fatimid ruler of Egypt, ordered the destruction of Christian and Jewish sanctuaries in 1012, and the Church of the Holy Sepulchre, among others, fell prey to his zeal. Still, Jerusalem never became wholly Moslem, and in the last quarter of the tenth century al-Muqaddasi, a Jerusalem-born geographer, noted that Christians and Jews had the upper hand in his native city. A similar situation probably existed in Bethlehem and Nazareth as well. But with the exception of these three cities, four hundred years of Moslem domination had made Syria and Palestine into Arabic-speaking, Moslem countries. And Islam added its claim to the Holy Land and its Holy Places to the growing list. The right was based on dominion and possession, but it was anchored in faith and religious exegesis.

Yet there was still another pretender to the Holy Land – one with no military forces, no imperial resources and yet the most persistent and enduring claimant of all – the Jew. Three times daily, the Jew expressed his nostalgia for the Holy Land and its capital, his hope of return and salvation. His claim was neither prescriptive nor alienable. The ardent faith which had preserved the dispersed nation for over a millennium linked the fulfilment of the prophecy of the end of days to that of the ingathering of the exiles and return to the homeland. Every great event in history, every turmoil and upheaval, was regarded as the forerunner of national salvation. In medieval Jewish eschatology, Byzantium was identified with vicious Edom (Idumea), and its fall was supposed to be the prelude to liberation. When Byzantium survived the Persians, it was successively the rise of Islam (622), the revolution of the Abbaside dynasty (750) and the victories of the Seljuq Turks (1071) which signalled the imminence of redemption. But each glittering promise ended in dashed hopes and broken hearts. Still, one was sure that just around the corner, around the very next bend, Providence would keep its promise to Israel.

It was under Byzantine rule, between the end of the fourth and the beginning of the seventh century, that Palestine became predominantly non-Jewish, either as a result of conversions to Christianity or migration of Jews to the Diaspora. Byzantium celebrated the triumph of its faith with anti-Jewish legislation and the formal prohibition against Jews living in the Holy City. Henceforth the pious pilgrim could only contemplate the city and the heaps of garbage accumulated on the Temple esplanade. So the Jew repeated his prayers from the height of the Mount of Olives, tore his vestments (as one did in sign of mourning) and hoped for better times. The Persian invasion of Palestine in AD 614 was the hour of vengeance, and revolted Jews participated in the onslaught that left Jerusalem in ashes. But Byzantium reaffirmed its rule, and for another generation the Jew was again barred from the city. The extent of Christian enmity towards the Jews was exemplified when Sophronius, the last Byzantine patriarch of Jerusalem, insisted that the Moslem conquerors perpetuate the discrimination and forbid Jews to settle in the Holy City.

Bypassing the prohibition, the first Jews settled near the Mosque of al-Aqsa as servants of the Moslem sanctuary. Once their presence was established, a Jewish quarter grew up near the Omayyad palace, and as their numbers grew another, more spacious quarter developed between the Damascus Gate and the Gate of Josaphat. Soon the Palestinian Academy, the revered seat of Jewish sages, moved from Tiberias to Jerusalem, though the demographic centre of Jewish life up to the eve of the Crusades was the newly built Moslem capital of Ramle on the coastal plain.

Thus the Holy Land, the Promised Land of three religions, remained the land of permanent claimants. Actual rule over the country at any one time was the result of specific historical circumstances; but its place in the hearts of men was a corollary of their most sublime emotions. At the end of the eleventh century, a unique constellation of political, cultural and religious factors combined to move one of the pretenders, Western Christendom, to translate its emotional bond with the Holy Land into political hegemony. The means to achieve this somewhat unexpected end was one of the boldest military campaigns in history and was followed by close to two hundred years of subsequent warfare, known by the generic term the Crusades.

2

The Crusade

Clermont, 27 November 1095. The pope's visit to the Burgundian city in the kingdom of France was nearing its end. The pontiff, Urban II, had convoked a council to discuss the reform of the French church, which – like all others – was afflicted with 'Simony' (lay interference in ecclesiastical matters). And no less pressing a topic was one of the current scandals of Christendom: despite the fulminations of the clergy, the Capetian king of France, Philip I, was living in sin with another man's wife. Behind the scenes, however, the pope was toying with a new idea: a crusade to liberate the Holy Sepulchre from the yoke of Islam.

The idea had actually been raised a generation earlier by Gregory VII. Moslem pressure in the Iberian Peninsula, as well as the menacing conquests of the Seljuq Turks (who captured Baghdad in 1055 and forayed into the Moslem territories of Syria and Palestine, and Byzantine Asia Minor), made the pontiff sharply aware of an all-menacing Moslem danger. He appealed for Christian aid in Spain and for a Christian expedition to repulse the Turks threatening Constantinople. In a flight of fancy, Gregory VII saw himself leading the liberation armies to the East. Papal leadership of a pan-Christian army to rescue Constantinople from the Infidel could spectacularly proclaim papal hegemony in Christian Europe, as well as the pope's newly assumed standing as defender of the faith, a role traditionally associated with the empire. This resounding gesture was a showman's argument. But there was more to it than met the eye. The Greek Church, which severed relations with the Holy See when Rome and Constantinople reciprocally anathematised each other (1054), might make amends were its capital to be saved by an army led by the head of western Christendom. The healing of the schism – as there were really no weighty dogmatic differences between East and West – seemed to be at hand. But the plan foundered in the stormy confrontation between papacy and empire.

Nonetheless, Constantinople did receive a contingent of heavy-mailed Western cavalry, and in 1094 an imperial embassy sent by Alexius I Comnenus appeared before the pope in Piacenza on the eve of his departure for Clermont. During the pope's journey to Clermont through southern France, a land aware of the fight against Islam in the neighbouring Iberian Peninsula, the idea of rescuing the Christian East matured but also altered in the process. From the idea of saving oriental Christendom (which was not in mortal danger at the time) it became the idea of liberating the Holy Sepulchre from the yoke of Islam. The new plan integrated earlier elements, but by fixing this new aim the papal declaration became an appeal for a crusade.

Constantinople was replaced by Jerusalem; but the enemy was the same Turks who ruled Asia Minor, threatened Constantinople and were now the masters of the Holy City.

The change to Jerusalem altered more than the geographical aim of the crusade; it changed its very character. From a detachment of mailed knights to be sent to the East it became a mass movement which for the next two hundred years would become a major focus of European and Near Eastern history. It was not the prestigious name of Constantinople but the venerated names Jerusalem, Nazareth and Bethlehem which stirred the imagination of millions, created a mes-sianic longing and exploded into a religious frenzy. The major objectives of the papacy – relations with the Roman Empire, the Eastern Empire and the Greek schismatic church – counted for little or nothing in the thoughts and emotions of the countless knights and peasants who joined the crusade. It was ideas and slogans like the liberation of Jerusalem and the liberation of the Sepulchre of the Saviour, whom one imagined was a prisoner in Moslem captivity, to which European Christianity enthusiastically responded.

The pope promised absolution to all who joined the crusade. Thus the concepts of pilgrimage and penitence joined forces with a new enterprise, a military expedition with a religious aim. Contrition and the dangers of the road were the penance imposed by the Church on a repentant sinner. Urban II recognised the crusade as equivalent to a penitential pilgrimage, which afforded the absolution from temporary punishment for sin. The crusade became a penitential *and martial* pilgrimage, and its goal was the Holy Sepulchre and prayer at the liberated tomb of the Saviour. No one, not even Urban II, could have foreseen the results of the appeal from Clermont. A host of knights, a well-organised military expedition, was envisaged and expected. But what actually happened surpassed men's wildest imagination. For two full years it seemed that all of Europe was on the move; a second great exodus to the Holy Land. One can hardly speak about a single motive or motivation where hundreds of thousands of people are concerned. Yet it cannot be doubted that the dominant motive behind the crusade was the religious one. Knights and princes joined the crusade to fulfil the obligation of their rank in the hierarchy of Christendom; burgesses and peasants sought their salvation. Still, one was not oblivious to the drawing power of the East and its marvels. Heavenly and earthly Jerusalem intermingled, as did the spiritual and material aspirations of men and mankind. Only a few months after word went out, the tidings had reached every corner of Christendom. The few who participated in the meeting at Clermont were the first bearers of the news, but in a short time the machinery of the Church – the most efficient and elaborate organisation of its age – became the propaganda medium for the new enterprise. The call from Clermont was diffused through church and monastery into every castle and village. It stirred the imagination, became a subject of conversation and created a climate of public opinion, which turned out to be a major factor in the history of the crusade. Lords of castles deliberated with their vassals and followers; princes looked around for means to finance the expedition; and from these summits of society the news filtered down into the humble dwellings of the peasants and the crowded housing of the nascent cities. The young squire and the bachelor dreamed about the marvels of the East: riches, palaces and the beauties of the harems. The younger sons of noble families – the young bloods – looked to the East as the Promised Land of their destinies. And yet the lust for adventure or the prospect of material rewards were only of secondary appeal to the nobility. Medieval men were basically religious, almost always superstitious and credulous. Whatever their knowledge of the dogmas of religion, the holy narrative was a part of their upbringing. Communion and confession, saints and their relics and great and solemn festivities of the Christian calendar were not only religious rites, but part of their life style. Answering the call to liberate the Saviour's sepulchre – an appeal stressed by the circulation of monstrous (and unfounded) stories

Earthly Jerusalem, the prefiguration of the Heavenly City, was the goal of pilgrimage and crusade. This realistic representation of buildings in a fantastic setting is from a 14th-century French illuminated manuscript (1)

above The glory that was Rome became the legacy of Christian Byzantium.
This detail of a mosaic in Hagia Sophia, Constantinople, shows Christ blessing
(in Greek fashion) Constantine IX and his empress, Zöe (2)

opposite The Christian *reconquista* moved from Spain through the
Mediterranean islands to the Holy Land. Spanish knights in action (3)

below Islam, the religion of the tribes of Arabia, became the faith of an empire
from Gibraltar to India. In this Turkish illumination, Mohammed (centre)
holds court with the patriarchs and prophets, among them Moses and Jesus (4)

The Jews never forgot
the promise given their
forefathers to inherit
the Holy Land which
was never abrogated
or alienated. Jews in
oriental garb from a
12th-century mosaic in
the cathedral of
Monreale, Sicily (5)

about the profanation of the Holy Places – was considered not only a duty of the noble-born Christian, but also a part of his chivalrous obligations, the duty of the feudal vassal to defend his Lord and liberate him from the cruel captivity of the sacrilegious Infidel. The basic piety of a religious age, amalgamated with the nascent ideas of knighthood, made Western nobility responsive to the pontiff's appeal for a crusade.

To some degree, the response of Western nobility could have been anticipated; but no one could have foreseen the reaction of the masses. The council of Clermont took place at the end of November, when the peasants were preparing for the winter. By the spring of 1096 the countryside was in an uproar. The peasants did not harvest for their next year's existence, but gathered their crops for the journey to the East. Some months later countless peasant families in thousands of hamlets loaded their meagre belongings, wives and children on heavy ox- or horse-drawn carts and took the road to the East. The story that upon hearing Urban II's call at Clermont thousands responded *Dieu le veut* ('God wills it') is probably untrue. But to the European peasantry, the pontiff's call sounded like a command directly from the Lord, the first miracle in a chain of events that presaged the Second Coming. The clerical chroniclers, who were familiar with the population, could not ascribe the sudden religious mood to anything short of a miracle. What else could move the apathetic, illiterate and materialistic masses?

No doubt many a peasant loading his family on his wagon thought not only about the salvation of his soul or the liberation of the Saviour's sepulchre, but also of his own liberation from serfdom and bondage. It was tacitly accepted that the lord of a manor would not prevent his serfs from leaving their land, and it was an established rule that the liberation army would be a host of free men. *Franci* not only denoted Frenchmen and, afterwards, all Europeans; it also meant free men. In the Holy Land, once the country was conquered, the warriors would remain free; the emigrant would be the proprietor of his own farm, perhaps of even a manor with a servile Moslem peasantry. And yet, though each might have had his own little hope and man-size greed, one cared for his own salvation and his immortal soul. The movement was to the East, in the direction of the altars, the rising sun, the eternal symbols of hope and salvation.

It was at the beginning of the eleventh century that Europe entered a period of religious awakening. The Last Judgement, expected (and dreaded) at the turn of the millennium – thirty-four years later (1034), a thousand years after the Crucifixion – stirred a wave of repentance in Central and Western Europe. The sense of sin and feeling of guilt deepened. The activities of Cluny, of reformed monasteries and finally of the reformed church itself added a new dimension to the religious climate. Religiously inspired movements made themselves felt even in the political life of the West, as for example the movements of Peace of God and Truce of God, which curbed local bloodshed. Fighting was limited, under threat of anathema and collective resistence, to particular days in the week, and the sufferings of the common people reasserted peace against the robber barons and adventurers. At the same time, the traumatic experience at the turn of the century caused men to look for means of liberation from the burden of sin. Hence the pilgrimages to holy shrines, the great appeal of monastic life and the revival of monasticism at the turn of the eleventh century, when a large number of new monastic orders sprung up in Italy and across the Alps. Nothing was more symptomatic than the first movements which preached the return to the poverty of the primitive Christian community – movements dangerous to the establishment and condemned as heretical by the Church. Yet not all was condemned. Here and there wandering preachers called for a *Vita Apostolica*, the return to following in the footsteps of the Apostles, and apostolic poverty was praised and declared to be a virtue. The imitation of their simple way of life was as much repentance for the past as a safeguard for the future.

The call to a crusade, which was prompted by far different reasons, suddenly became a call for a collective act of penance, a panacea for the needs and woes of the generation. Freedom from the oppressive feeling of sin and infernal punishment hereafter; the chance to fight with the approval of fellow men and the blessing of the Church; the opportunity to discharge one's obligation as a Christian and a knight and to reach the earthly Jerusalem, which seemed to call to its true sons to deliver her from the Infidel, an earthly victory with a promise of heavenly reward – all these pointed the way to the East.

And after the conquest? Nobody, strange as it seems, had even asked the question. If Urban II or Adhemar, bishop of Le Puy, his nominee as the leader of the crusade, had any clear ideas, they did not make them public. Perhaps some of the princes had plans, but they too kept their counsel, as nothing was known of them until the Crusader armies reached the soil of Asia Minor. For the great mass of peasants, burghers, clergymen, monks and knights, the goal was to reach Jerusalem. It was no coincidence that the common people participating in the crusade showed unheard of signs of self-assurance, even haughtiness. If the Day of Judgement was near, were not they, the poorest, the first – according to the Scriptures – to enter heavenly Jerusalem? The poor therefore became a distinctive class, an estate. Some would even associate only in a curiously exclusive company of have-nots, a group who felt themselves already elected and saved.

Thus in the spring and summer of 1096, just half a year after the epoch-making speech at Clermont, the peasant precursors of the great Knights' Crusade were on the move. Single families joined others, and groups on their march to the Rhine swelled into bands and hosts. Some chose leaders from among their peers; others accepted a knight or a member of a local noble family; still others moved without any leadership. One host was even led by a goat or a goose; but this did not make it ridiculous, as the goose was a symbol of magic and there was no doubt that the divine movement was directed by super-natural forces. Those who doubted had only to hear about the voices, dreams and visions of the elected ones, local prophets who enjoyed their moments of glory.

What began as an upsurge of religious feeling, the march of the Militant Church to the accompaniment of psalmody, was quickly marred by one of the greatest atrocities in history: the blood-curdling massacre and annihilation of the Jewish communities in the Rhineland. Some of these communities had originated in the Roman Empire before any German barbarian set foot on this Celtic soil. Others were younger, and some of these had been established on the formal request and invitation of local bishops who wanted to populate the embryonic cities and turn them into centres of commerce and revenue. The Jewish communities flourished, and in the eleventh century a great school of the Sages of Sarfath (France) and Lothar (Lorraine) created the first great works of biblical and talmudic exegesis in northern Europe. Then struck the catastrophe which is comparable only to the holocaust of our own times. In a frenzy of messianic excitement, the unruly, popular masses of the crusade placed before the Jews the choice of apostasy or death. The communities chose martyrdom. Even a cynical age can hardly read descriptions of the massacres without revulsion. Hatred of the Jews, more or less latent in all countries of Christendom, found an outlet in pogroms, a phenomenon which would become an integral part of almost every crusade during the two hundred years of the movement. Entire Jewish communities were wiped out, and thousands of Jews who refused to be baptised were slaughtered. Two generations later, during the Second Crusade (1147), a new awe-inspiring rite evolved in the communities, the rite of martyrdom. Rather than undergo forced baptism, men cut the throats of their wives and children while reciting the prayer for slaughtering animals and then committed suicide. The crusaders who penetrated the Jewish hide-outs found silent courtyards filled with the corpses of those who testified to the truth of their religious convictions. In a few months flourishing communities disappeared and centres of learning and culture – Speyer, Worms, Cologne, Prague – were destroyed. More-over, the social standing of the communities was compromised, and the Jew embarked upon the long centuries of darkness and persecution which in many places lasted to the threshold of the twentieth century.

Here and there a bishop tried to save the Jews. Official Church policy prohibited forced baptism or the massacre of Jews, who were to be preserved as witnesses of the faith. Their degradation, it was argued, should stand as ever-present testimony to the victory of the Church Triumphant. But intervention of prelates was almost never effective. The excited masses found the hiding places (often castles), stormed them and put the Jews to the sword. They proclaimed that before fighting the Infidel abroad, one had to clean his own house. Names of commanders like Volkmar, Gottschalk and Emicho, other-wise unrecorded in Western history, were added to the long list of infamy in the history of the nation of martyrs.

The masses which crossed the Rhine turned south to the Danube and proceeded eastwards. Undisciplined and excited, given to fears and suspicions, they soon ran out of provision and began looting. In France, Germany and even Bohemia, the local population supplied them with food; but in Hungary and the Balkans the marching bands behaved like an invading army in an enemy territory. The Hungarians organised armed resistance and entered into pitched battles with the marauding companies. The situation became even worse when they entered the Balkans, that is, the territory of the Byzantine Empire. An unknown language, a different church and strange customs turned the encounter of Eastern and Western Christianity into a military campaign. The Byzantines sent troops, often Turks in their service, to curb the bands.

They even supplied food to prevent plunder. But the road to Constantinople was marked by burnt villages, plundered cities and heaps of corpses. Byzantium, which the Western host was supposed to succour, fell victim to their excesses.

Hunger, sickness and local resistance decimated the popular crusade. Of the many bands which moved out from Europe, only ragged remnants reached Constantinople. One of them was led by Peter the Hermit, or Peter of Amiens, whom a later legend made the great hero of the Crusades. Though he had more influence than most over the unruly masses, he did not succeed in retaining them in the capital. By then Alexius I Comnenus and his subjects had had enough. The emperor quickly transported them across the Bosporus, where they finally faced the Moslems. Totally unprepared and undisciplined, they dispersed around ancient Nicaea, where they suffered tremendous losses at the hands of the Turks. Only the intervention of the emperor succeeded in saving some bands and bringing them back to the safety of the capital. At the beginning of the autumn of 1096, the Peasants' Crusade came to its fatal end.

While the popular crusade was petering out in the passes of the Balkans and ended pitfully just outside the walls of Constantinople, the great Knights' Crusade was gathering momentum. Better organised and infinitely more disciplined, the knightly hosts of Western Europe began moving in the mid-summer of 1096. The French-speaking rulers of England joined their brethren and relatives across the channel in France; the Knights of Flanders joined hosts from northern and central France. Knights from northern Italy prepared for the crusade; and in the south of the peninsula, the Normans, still busy fighting Moslems and Byzantines to carve out a Norman kingdom on both sides of the Straits of Messina, threw in their lot with the crusade. But neither Spain – busy with its own Moslems – nor Germany – in the midst of the Investiture Contest – answered the pope's call. The distant Scandinavians moved on a little later, and a small trickle of Slavs from Bohemia and Poland and Magyars from Hungary participated in later crusades.

All in all, four large armies concentrated. Their composition was based on geographical divisions and local, ethnic or linguistic loyalties. Duke Robert of Normandy led the hosts of north-western France, joined by the subjects of his brother Henry I of England. Godfrey of Bouillon led the army of Flanders, Lorraine and north-western France;

Hugh of Vermandois, brother of King Philip I of France, led the Knights of central France, the homeland of the Capetian dynasty. Raymond of St Gilles, count of Toulouse and marquis of Provence, headed the host of southern France, Provence and Languedoc up to the confines of the Pirenees. Finally, Bohemond of Otranto and his more famous nephew Tancred took their places at the head of the Italian Normans.

Adhemar de Monteuil, bishop of Le Puy, was appointed as a kind of pope's representative. As the highest-ranking prelate, he also became a co-ordinator and mediator between the leaders. The great hosts, though composed primarily of knights, were joined by a great number of simple people, predominantly peasants who usually moved with their traditional local chiefs. Excesses happened here and there, but as a whole the armies moved with a relatively satisfactory degree of order. The French contingents took the overland route to the East through the Rhineland and the Danube basin, whereas those of Norman Italy and some from France crossed the Adriatic Sea and moved through the ancient Roman Via Egnatia across the Balkans.

The rallying point was Constantinople, where the armies met and concentrated in the spring of 1097. This was their first meeting with the East, the oriental Christian empire on the Bosporus. None of the participants could possibly have conjured up the sight of the great capital. Coming from a 'city-less' Europe, where the greatest urban agglomerations numbered several tens of thousands at most and the smaller ones hardly ever reached five thousand, the crusaders marvelled at the beauty of the capital, its mile-long walls, skyline of gilded cupolas, churches and palaces, bazaars and market-places, bustling port and monuments of classical glory. But above all, they were awed by the great masses of inhabitants. This was the gateway, a magnificent introduction to the mysterious and enchanted East. And this was also the moment of the first clash with the claims of Byzantium.

Emperor Alexius I Comnenus, a vigorous ruler who tried to make the best of the defeat of the Byzantine Army at the hands of the Seljuq Turks at Manzikert one generation earlier (1070), could not help but be overwhelmed by the arrival of his 'saviours'. Not only were they not the regiment of cavalry he expected, but the pitiful and unruly remnants of the Peasants' Crusade had led him to anticipate the worst. Faced by the bleak prospect of seeing his empire left to the mercy of stronger and larger European armies, the emperor tried to come to some kind of an understanding with the leaders. It was out of the question to treat them as a mercenary army to be put on his pay-roll and employed in his service; but it was equally difficult to regard them as allies. Fortunately, the different hosts did not arrive simultaneously, which gave the emperor the opportunity to deal with the leaders individually. Moreover, Raymond of St Gilles and Bohemond of Otranto (a redoubtable ally who some years earlier had invaded the Byzantine Balkans), aspired to a kind of imperial lieutenancy which would strengthen their position among the Crusader leaders. Using ruse, threats and bribery, the emperor succeeded in extracting from them a promise to safeguard the rights of his empire in their future conquests within former Byzantine territory. Ultimately, almost all commanders took an oath to the emperor, and the latter supplied them with guides, money and provisions and transported them with alacrity across the straits to the Asian mainland.

It was there, a few miles outside Constantinople, that the crusaders found themselves in enemy territory for the first time. After the Turkish victory at Manzikert, the whole of Asia Minor was in their hands. However, the new Turkish domination had not yet changed the composition of the population, which remained overwhelmingly Byzantine, and only the castles and city citadels were manned by the Seljuq garrisons. If there was any sense in the slogan of liberation, therefore, it was here that the crusaders had to prove it.

At first it seemed that things would work out well for the Christian host. The city of Nicaea was besieged and capitulated, at the request of the besieged, to Byzantium. The Crusader armies moved southwards and achieved victory in the memorable battle at the pass of Dorylaeum (in 1097). All organised resistance ceased throughout Asia Minor, though the hosts were exposed to constant attacks à la turque, when units of swift-riding archers, seemingly appearing out of nowhere, would suddenly attack, discharge their arrows and disappear as suddenly as they had come. These unpredictable attacks were painful but could not stop the onward movement of the armies. Their chief enemies became the climate, the heat of central Asia Minor, and when they ran out of provisions generously supplied by the Byzantine emperor, the lack of food and water. But the armies struggled southwards, then changed their course and, describing a large area, turned into the interior, towards the heart of Asia Minor. Then they continued to the south up to the passage between the majestic massive of the

Taurus Mountains. On their way the crusaders captured Iconium (Qoniya), the capital of the Seljuq Turks in Asia Minor.

Reaching the Taurus Mountains, the crusaders met the Christians of what was to become known as Lesser Armenia, a population which had migrated there a century earlier from Greater Armenia around Lake Van and found new political cohesion in local principalities. It was also there that the crusaders received their first call for help from a Christian population. The vicissitudes of war and conquest had created a large belt, from the sea in the west far into Upper Mesopotamia in the east, of small principalities whose population was often Christian, Armenian and Monophysite Jacobites. Some were ruled by former Byzantine officers, others by renegade Byzantines or Armenians, paying tribute or homage – or both – to the Turkish commanders or governors of their districts. It was from such a Christian population in and around Edessa that an appeal for help reached the crusaders. Baldwin, the brother of Godfrey of Bouillon, moved to their rescue. He was hailed as liberator and adopted as a son by the ruler of Edessa; but fomenting a revolt against his benefactor, Baldwin took over the city and created the first Crusader principality in the East, the County of Edessa. The emblem of the ducal house of Lorraine was planted between the Tigris and Euphrates, and Europe had established its first colony overseas.

In the meantime, the Crusader host crossed the Taurus passes and entered northern Syria. The centres of Moslem government were in Antioch and Damascus. Since Antioch's conquest by the Turks in 1085, Syria had been split up into small emirates which recognised the Abbaside caliph of Baghdad and the suzerainty of the Seljuq sultan in distant Persia. In reality, fighting among the emirs was almost constant.

The crusaders invested Antioch in the first regular and prolonged siege of the First Crusade (1097–8). Despite valiant defence, the city fell through the treachery of an Armenian renegade. The capture of Antioch saved the crusade as a large Seljuq army from Mosul moved to the city's rescue and was only few days' march away. Had the city not fallen, the exhausted and starving Crusader host, caught between the Moslem city and the relief troops, would have ended its days on the Orontes.

opposite The sultan's guard from an illuminated manuscript of al-Hariri's *Maqamat*

ويحلل الفصّ والجبّة والفرس والدار بالله انها لصّغت على بالله فأضاعت بفضل مربحها
ونشد منزرها فلما قرت أنسى بالرقعة درهما وقطعة وقلت لها ان رغبت فى المستوفى المعلم
واشرت الى الدرهم فوحى بالسرّ المنهم وان ابيت ان نترجى خذى فى القطعة وايرجى

لان الى اسطلاص البدر بالنير والأبلج الهرم وقالت جد ذلك ونابعما بذلك فاسطط
لغ الشيخ ولدنه والشعر وابيح بردته فقالت ان الشيخ من اهل شروج وهو الذى وثى

Failing to rescue Antioch, Karbuqa's army then settled in to besiege the crusaders, who shut themselves up within the city and suffered badly in the cadaver-infested and famished capital. It seemed that only a miracle could save them, and a miracle there was. An obscure Provençal cleric was granted a heavenly apparition announcing that the lance which had pierced the body of Christ eleven hundred years earlier was hidden in Antioch. As the apparition had pointed out the exact spot, the Holy Lance was easily found. This heavenly sign heightened the morale of the army, and its courage found expression in a sortie against the besieging Moslems which carried the day. The defeated Turkish army disbanded and disappeared. There was no other Moslem army which could have barred the way to earthly Jerusalem; but there was human greed.

The long road, maladies and deprivations which had culminated in incredible sufferings during the double siege of Antioch brought about moral disorganisation and what may be described as the ideological bankruptcy of the crusade. The pent-up greed and cravings, tempered until then by both ideology and grim reality, broke out at the moment of respite in a pandemonium of quarrels and intrigues among the Crusader leaders. Bohemond, the architect of the victory at Antioch, was challenged by Raymond of St Gilles's claim to the city, but the leaders of the host decided to leave Antioch to the Norman and, incidentally, to ignore the agreement with the Byzantine emperor, who claimed the capital of Syria as his own. In the wake of this dispute, the Crusader host simply disbanded. The leaders, chiefs, and lesser knights alike, forayed from Antioch into the surrounding countryside, each trying to carve out a domain for himself. Local resistance was feeble, and villages, cities and castles became Frankish. Westerners found Syrian lodgings comfortable and the food delicious. The stay in northern Syria began to look permanent. One had the impression that Antioch had replaced Jerusalem and the Orontes, the Jordan. But just at that point an unexpected popular revolt challenged the leadership. The poor still bore the torch of the original ideology and called their leadership to order. Their spokesmen boldly announced that the aim of the crusade was not to create domains for the leaders; that the goal was not Antioch, but Jerusalem. Initially received with astonishment and ridicule, the mockery turned into shock when the leaders of the revolt threatened to burn Antioch and demolish its walls if the leaders did not move on instantaneously to Jerusalem.

This time the reaction was equal to the threat. The Crusader leaders took a solemn oath never to forget Jerusalem and after repentance the army moved out into southern Syria and Lebanon. The Moslem centres east of the Orontes River, Aleppo, Hama and Homs, made no effort to stop its progress. Moreover, the emirs of the coastal cities facilitated its movement and supplied the army with provisions in order to rid themselves of the invaders. And indeed, in their eagerness to reach Jerusalem, the crusaders did not stop to capture cities or castles, with the exception of Lebanese Tripoli, which was unsuccessfully besieged and left to a small observation garrison. In the spring of 1099, the army bypassed some of the most resounding names of the ancient and hellenistic worlds – Beirut, Sidon, Tyre – and finally reached Palestine proper. Following the coast of Galilee, the army contoured the bay of Acre, entered the fertile Sharon Plain of biblical fame and continued up to Caesarea. Then, before reaching the port of Jaffa, it turned inland to Ramle and neighbouring Lydda, where the army rested for a few days and consecrated its first bishop in the Holy Land, the bishop of St George (i.e., Lydda), as a kind of first fruits offering to the God of the hosts in His Promised Land.

The crusaders should have been more grateful than they realised. The panic-stricken Moslems abandoned the port of Jaffa, as well as Ramle, without a fight. After the capture of Jerusalem these two localities would assure the crusaders a half-way shelter and direct outlet to the sea. The entire future of the crusades depended on reinforcements and supplies from Europe, and these came over the seas.

After a three-day rest, the army stationed a garrison in Ramle, and engaged itself into the Mountains of Judea. On 7 June 1099 the crusaders reached the top of a hill overlooking Jerusalem, the traditional burial place of the prophet Samuel, and, finally, laid eyes on the Holy City. The hill was baptised as 'Montjoie', the Hill of Joy. The army knelt down in prayer and contemplated the hallowed city, with its domes and minarets, flat-roofed houses and round-topped bazaars. One could hardly distinguish the dome of the Church of the Resurrection, which had been restored two generations earlier. Behind the city, on the horizon, was the Mount of Olives and the place of the Lord's Ascension. The crusade was nearing its end. A Christian delegation from Bethlehem arrived and asked for protection, as Moslem fanaticism and desire for vengeance threatened their existence. Tancred rode out at night, and on the next morning a Norman banner floated over the

Church of the Nativity – before any Westerner had entered the holy city of Jerusalem.

The last chapter of the crusade was the five-week siege of Jerusalem (7 June–15 July 1099). Surrounded on all sides but the north by deep valleys, the city was prepared for a prolonged siege. The crusaders established their camps all along the northern, western and southern walls of the city, but they were unable to enclose the city from the east (that is, between the Temple esplanade and the Mount of Olives). They envisaged a regular siege, but it soon became obvious that their forces would hardly be able to carry out the task.

Nothing could be more appropriate to the atmosphere of this final episode in the epic of the First Crusade than the recurrence of heavenly apparition and the participation of St George in the battles. Here were the leaders of the crusade, heroes of a hundred battles, veteran warriors, asking advice of a hermit who lived in one of the caves of the Mount of Olives on how to capture the city. The futile assaults on the walls, the barefooted procession around them, the expectation that they would crumble like those of Jericho – all in vain. It took five weeks until the siege machines were ready, and a general attack was launched on a Friday, 15 July 1099. At noon, the traditional hour of Crucifixion, the siege tower of Godfrey of Bouillon succeeded in approaching the eastern end of the north wall. A bridge was lowered to the top of the battlements, and the host penetrated the city through the Jewish Quarter. At the same time Raymond of St Gilles, at the south-western corner (Mount Zion), penetrated the city and received the capitulation of the Egyptian commander of the citadel, while Tancred moved directly to the Dome of the Rock.

The fall of Jerusalem was followed by an atrocious massacre of the Moslem and Jewish defenders and population. The city was sacked for three consecutive days. Blood flowed in the streets, and heaps of corpses would infest them for a long time after. Then, in the deadly silence and stench of burned houses and rotting corpses, the crusaders gathered in the Church of Resurrection. *Te Deum laudamus* reverberated in the ancient Byzantine basilica. The crusade had come to an end; the Crusader kingdom was founded.

3

The Cross and the Crescent

Jerusalem was Christian. After four hundred years of Moslem domination, the cross had replaced the crescent. Mosques and synagogues were converted into churches; the *mihrab* (the niche in the southern wall facing Mecca) was walled up, and altars were installed in the direction of the rising sun. Infidels – Moslems and Jews alike – were banned from settling in the Holy City, as the conquerors deemed it sacrilegious to permit those who rejected the Christian Messiah to live in the place of His Passion and Crucifixion.

In the last days of the eleventh century, there was a Christian capital in the Holy Land. Small Frankish colonies were precariously established in Edessa, Mesopotamia, Antioch, Syria and a few cities on the Lebanese coast. These centers, few and far between, had to be linked in order to create a territorially compact state. The task seemed overwhelming, but a glance back at the epic of the First Crusade, with its spectacle of tortuous roads to its final victory, could be comforting. *Dieu le veut* had been the warcry of the crusade. Providence wished to purify its abode; saints had participated in battle and brought victory to the hosts of the True Faith; there was hope for the future.

That the Crusader kingdom had come to stay was a bitter, unexpected reality which faced Islam at the close of the eleventh century. Slowly but inexorably the crusaders' precarious hold on a few, scattered cities and castles turned into domination of compact territories, which continued to expand with little or no opposition. Islam was panic stricken. The Syrian emirates of Aleppo, Shaizar, Hama, Homs and Damascus – ruled by the Seljuq Turks or by local dynasties all acknowledging the sovereignty of the Abbaside caliphate in Baghdad – were paralysed. The fratricidal wars of the decade before the Crusader invasion had left a scar of bitterness, jealousy and suspicion. The gulf which divided the perpetually warring emirates of the north from the competitive Moslem south was so deep that for some time no common action could be envisaged. Egypt, the great Moslem power ruled by the Shi'ite caliphate of the Fatimids, was a religious, economic and political rival of Syria and Baghdad. The division between the Sunnites of Baghdad and Shi'ites of Cairo was not only a difference in religious tenets. Each caliphate claimed exclusive legitimacy and accused the other of usurpation and heterodoxy. Moreover, within Syria, Mesopotamia and even distant Persia, whence the Seljuq sultan supposedly ruled the Moslem orthodox empire, a variety of conflicting vested interests prevented the mobilisation of Islam's great economic and demographic resources.

This political disarray encouraged the crusaders and enabled them to reach Jerusalem. Their luck held for almost two generations, a span of time which allowed them to consolidate their conquests. In the face of the stronger and richer powers of Islam, the crusaders nonetheless created a state which held its own for two hundred years.

The first conquests after the capture of Jerusalem were along the vital Mediterranean Shore. The coast was not just another front of expansion, but an indispensable requisite for the survival of the embryonic Crusader establishments. Their very existence depended on the flow of reinforcements from Europe, which was brimming over with new waves of warriors and emigrants, ready to follow in the victorious footsteps of the First Crusade. Several attempts (1100–2) to follow the land route of the First Crusade ended in disaster, and the road was abandoned until the Second and then again the Third Crusade. The closing of the land route via Asia Minor by the Seljuqs of the sultanate of Rum (Iconium) left no other route but the sea. In the beginning no more than two ports were in Crusader hands: St Simeon, the port of Antioch, and the rather treacherous port of Jaffa, which had been abandoned by the Moslems when the crusaders made their way to Ramle and Jerusalem. But the seaboard extended for some five hundred miles from Alexandretta (Iskenderun) to Gaza. The difficulties facing the crusaders were enormous. They could not starve out the cities which had their provisions constantly replenished from Damascene Tyre or, more likely, by the fleets of Egypt, to whom the cities nominally owed allegiance. Moreover, the crusaders had no fleet and no maritime experience whatsoever.

It was at this point that the navies of the young and vigorous Italian republics became instrumental in the conquest of Syria and

Palestine. Genoa first, then Pisa, followed by Venice, directed their
fleets to the Holy Land. For a whole decade, the Ligurian and Adriatic
seas witnessed the departure of fleets to the East, around Easter, to
reach the waters of the Levant in April or May. First without pre-
conceived plans, and later in co-ordination with the crusaders, the
Italian marines blockaded Moslem maritime cities from the sea, while
the crusaders maintained the siege on land. Whether taken by storm
or reduced to docile capitulation, the fate of all the coastal cities was
the same: they were overrun and sacked, their populations exterminated, sometimes in contravention of previous agreements.
For a whole decade the crusaders hammered unrelentingly at the fortified seaboard, and at the end of this period (1111) the whole Syro-
Lebanese-Palestinian coast was in Crusader hands. Only the strongly
fortified, peninsular Tyre held out until 1123 and the Egyptian city of
Ascalon until 1154. The conquest of the seaboard fixed the western,
natural frontier of the Crusader realm.

Although the conquest of the maritime cities was accomplished
in a short time, it was a strain on the never too powerful forces of the
young Crusader establishments. The conquest of the interior, however,
was relatively easy. This area was not strongly fortified; few cities
had walls and there were few castles because the Damascene rulers
had not regarded the province as a frontier territory. Thus, almost
immediately after the conquest of Jerusalem, Crusader leaders overran
northern Judea and Samaria without encountering opposition. Pushing
northwards, Tancred captured Mount Tabor, Nazareth and Tiberias,
imposing Crusader rule on Galilee. Once Tiberias was captured,
Crusader incursions continued across the Sea of Galilee and the Jordan
River into the Golan Heights and from there towards the great Moslem
capital of Syria, Damascus. Crusader forces were too small to be a real
threat to the great city. They were ridiculously too few for a siege
(in a few of the major incursions, some eighty knights took part).
However, continuous forays into the unfortified countryside, the
capture of grazing livestock, the destruction of crops and the flight of
the native population soon placed burdens on the capital in the form
of refugees, food shortages and rising prices.

These raiding parties, together with the attacks on the western
seacoast, began to etch the future map of the kingdom. By the beginning
of their second decade, the crusaders had crystallized a military and
political doctrine of security which can be summarized in the notion

of 'natural frontiers'. The northern frontier was friendly as it ran between Beirut (captured in 1110) and Gibelet (ancient Byblos) in the county of Tripoli (roughly modern Lebanon). To the north-east the crusaders dominated the sources of the Jordan, as well as the only stronghold in the area, the city of Baniyas (ancient Caesarea Philippi) and its citadel. The eastern frontier was more of a problem. Facing Damascus in the north, the crusaders could never mobilise enough strength either to capture the city or even to implant themselves in fortifications in the Golan. The Damascenes, for their part, saw their flourishing agriculture and pasture lands systematically destroyed by Crusader razzias, which they could neither prevent nor effectively oppose. It was practically impossible to build fortresses, because of the proximity of Crusader bases.

The result of the impasse was unexpected. As early as 1108, the crusaders and Damascenes agreed on a kind of condominium over the Golan. No frontier was actually established, but both parties agreed to keep the entire area demilitarised, to abstain from erecting fortifications there and to divide its income: one third to Damascus, one third to the crusaders and one third to the peasants who actually tilled the fields. This territory extended south to around the Yarmuk River, or, as far south as Damascus could effectively intervene. Across the Yarmuk, the lands nominally under Damascus' dominion were taken over by the crusaders. Beginning in 1115 they penetrated the ancient lands of Gilead and Ammon (that is, Transjordan). Despite its barrenness, this thinly populated pasture land played an important role in the strategy and economy of the Near East. Its geopolitical position at the cross-roads of Mesopotamia, Syria and the Hejaz and at the terminal of the Egyptian trans-Sinai road made the main desert road of the area into a major thoroughfare.

The scattered Moslem fortifications, beyond the effective reach of either Damascus or Egypt, were easily brought to their knees. It was here and not at the Jordan River – with its shallow fords – that the crusaders established their frontier. Starting from the transversal Yarmuk Valley, they erected a line of fortifications from Amman to 'Aqaba. Two huge castles, Crac of Moab and Shaubaq (renamed Montréal), and several smaller ones became the Crusader guardians of Transjordan. And although ten or so castles could not secure a 250-mile-long stretch of land, the location of the castles made up in quality what they lacked in numbers. The Transjordanian fortresses,

usually erected on the ruins of ancient castles, were strung out along
the only north–south highway of Transjordan. Armies or caravans to
Hejaz or Egypt from Damascus or Baghdad and back had to move
on this highway, and the fortified sites also served as watering places.
This route was also the famous *Darb al-Haj*, the 'Road of Pilgrimage'
leading to Mecca and Medina. The Crusader implantation in Transjordan consequently controlled one of the major commercial and
military arteries of Islam. Moreover, the strategic importance of the
'Road of Pilgrimage' increased when Syria was unified with Egypt
and their direct land link was cut by the Crusader wedge in Transjordan.

The policy of choosing natural frontiers (that is, the desert) to separate
the lands of the cross from those of the crescent became a major issue in
the south-western part of the Crusader kingdom. Effective Crusader
domination of the coast extended as far as Jaffa, which was the natural
port to serve Jerusalem, but was checked at Ascalon. This city of
ancient Philistine fame almost fell immediately after the capture of
Jerusalem; but the crusaders missed their chance, and it was not until
fifty-five years later, after two generations of painful attempts, that
Ascalon was captured. It was defended by an Egyptian garrison, and
its importance escaped neither the crusader nor the Egyptian command.
From the latter's point of view, Ascalon was a military outpost which
allowed for the concentration of provisions and forces in an excellent
base across the desert. From there it was easy to attack Hebron, Bethlehem, Ramle, or even Jaffa and cut Jerusalem off from the coast. In fact,
during the first decade of Crusader rule, the Egyptians sallied forth
several times a year into the plain of Ramle and Lydda. They were
never entirely successful, however, and their attacks on Jaffa failed for
lack of cooperation or timing between the garrison at Ascalon and the
Egyptian navy. To preserve Ascalon and assure fresh combative forces,
the Egyptians changed the city's garrison quarterly. As the crusaders
laid waste to its agricultural countryside, the Egyptians went as far
as enrolling every child born in the city on their military payroll.

Ascalon and the Ascalon strip became a thorn in the side of the kingdom, constantly threatening its security. The challenge was met by
creating a defence line, a kind of *cordon sanitaire*, around Ascalon on
all the main roads leading from it in the direction of Jaffa, Ramle and
Bethlehem. This curbed the Egyptian incursions, and the restoration
of Gaza in 1150 cut off Egypt's desert route to Ascalon across Sinai.
In 1154, during political and military difficulties in Cairo, the crusaders

The sense of sin and urge for repentance spread from the world of the monasteries to manor, village and castle. This 12th-century sculpture of a monk was executed in Italy (6)

On the roads to the Holy Shrines. One pilgrim returns from Santiago de Compostela, his scrip marked by a shell; the other from *Sancta Hierusalem*, the cross proclaiming his pilgrimage (7)

Dieu le veut! The crusade begins at God's command (8)

The poor on the roads: the Peasants' Crusade to Jerusalem (9)

Heavenly intervention during the crusaders' assault on Jerusalem. The hermit (at left) prophesies victory, while St. George looks down from the Mount of Olives (10)

right 15 July 1099. Friday, at the hour of the Crucifixion, the host of Godfrey of Bouillon scaled the walls of Jerusalem at this point and penetrated into the heart of the Holy City (11)

below Stones tell the story of the Basilica of Nativity in Bethlehem. Below the cornice of the Byzantine basilica, the romanesque arch evokes the Crusader era. The slab above the entrance dates from Ottoman times (12)

struck and captured Ascalon. The fall of the city and the fortification
of Gaza pushed the frontiers of the kingdom to the edge of the desert.

Even before the fall of Ascalon, the crusaders had probed deeply
into the desert itself. The oasis of el-Arish was destroyed several
times; expeditions even ventured as far as the eastern branch of the
Nile; but no tangible results were achieved. Still, Baldwin I, the valiant
Crusader king who tried to master the desert route to Egypt, was
memorialised in Sabkhat Bardawil, the marshy lake which bears
his name; and at the beginning of the twentieth century the Bedouins
of northern Sinai still told stories about the blond giant Bardawil.

As the Crusader kingdom reached its maximum extension and
attained its desert frontiers, Islam began to react to the Crusader challenge. The fifty years following the establishment of the kingdom had
proved that the Syrian emirates were unable to cooperate, let alone
create a common front. They also proved that Egypt, with all its
economic resources and manpower, was no match for the Europeans.
From time to time Syrian emirates did conclude agreements, even with
Egypt, casting an eye towards common action. But alliances were
broken as easily as they were concluded. The truth was that the emirs
were too suspicious of each other to join in a common front against the
crusaders. Once the frontiers between cross and crescent were established roughly along the great depression which extends from the
Taurus Mountains down to the Dead Sea (with the exception of the
Latin kingdom of Jerusalem, which included Transjordan), a kind of
an equilibrium was created.

The Moslem reaction did not originate in either Syria or Egypt,
however; it began in Mosul. The governors of Mosul owed allegiance
to the Seljuq sultan, whose seat was in Persia. They were his representatives in the western part of the empire and in this capacity supervised
the Syrian and Mesopotamian emirates, as well as the caliph of Baghdad
himself. It was in the name of caliph and sultan that they tried to get
some kind of cooperation from the Moslem rulers of Syria. Several
military expeditions, especially against their immediate Crusader
neighbours, in the county of Edessa and the principality of Antioch,
were launched at their initiative. But the results were seldom satisfactory
as the Moslem emirs suspected – and not without reason – the rulers
of Mosul of base designs on their autonomy and possessions. Still,
in 1113 a great military coalition led by the governor of Mosul won
a battle at Sinnabra, near the Sea of Galilee and besieged almost the

total force of the Crusader kingdom near Tiberias. Only their inability to keep a heterogeneous army in the field for a longer period deprived the Moslems of a resounding victory. This failure was made even more painful by the fact that the appearance of a large Moslem army in the Holy Land encouraged the native population to revolt against the crusaders and support what might be called a Moslem liberation army.

Despite the failure, however, something had begun to change in the camp of Islam. The influx of refugees into Moslem territory after the Crusader conquest stirred resentment against Moslem leadership. Initially the discontent was voiced from the *minbars*, the preaching chairs of the mosques, at the solemn Friday prayer; then the movement received stronger, popular support; and very soon the idea of the *jihad*, the Holy War against the Infidel, became the rallying cry of Moslem forces. The idea of the *jihad*, as old as Islam itself, had been dormant for centuries. Islam had accepted the coexistence with Christian Byzantium, as a matter of fact. The idea of a permanent war to establish the True Faith, like the modern idea of a permanent revolution to establish the only right and just political régime, remained exclusively in books. Now it was unearthed: treatises were written about the duty of waging the Holy War and pamphlets were circulated about the holiness of the city of Jerusalem.

This ideological stirring was exploited by one of the most gifted Moslem rulers, Zengi. With his support the *madrassas* (Moslem theological academies), ulemas and pietist circles created a climate of public opinion which made it more and more difficult for the Syrian emirs to evade direct confrontation with the challenge created by the Crusader kingdom. Step by step, Zengi succeeded, in overcoming the centrifugal forces in Mesopotamia and Syria, and in 1144 a successful attack against Edessa brought under his rule the capital of the first Crusader state established in the Orient.

The loss of Edessa was ominous, painful and a psychological shock. It meant that the principality of Antioch, Edessa's north-western neighbour, would have to bear permanent Moslem pressure on its frontiers. Moslem attacks would be more frequent now that the threat of a flanking Crusader attack from Edessa had been removed. An attempt to recover the city in 1146 ended in failure for the city was recaptured by a new rising star in Moslem politics, Nur el-Din, the heir and successor of Zengi. Despite his spectacular victory, however, Nur el-Din was unable to launch a full-fledged attack on the Crusader kingdom. His sovereignty over the Syrian and Mesopotamian emirates was still precarious and became even more so in the face of fierce opposition by Damascus. The capital of Syria had reached a *modus vivendi* with its Crusader neighbours which assured its political independence and economic standing. With time Damascus found the crusaders to be more reliable as neighbours, and on occasion as allies, than the nearby Moslems. The ruling dynasty of Damascus, which identified itself more with local interests than with Seljuq politics, did not want to be liberated, either by Zengi or Nur el-Din, only to see itself incorporated in the domains of the Zengids. Damascus preferred its independence, and for almost two generations the policy of the ruling dynasty enjoyed the support of the citizenry. Naturally enough, Damascus became the focus of anti-Zengid opposition. Under these conditions the crusaders more than once lent a helping hand to Damascus when threatened by Zengi and Nur el-Din. The latter could hardly attack the Latin kingdom with unreliable Damascus at his back, and the proximity of the crusaders prevented any prolonged siege of the Syrian capital.

Oddly enough the crusaders themselves undermined this propitious arrangement. The fall of Edessa became a major challenge to Christian Europe. It was unnatural and unjust that a Christian state should be conquered by Infidels; that the True Faith had lost in the confrontation. Europe was moved by a feeling of shame, vengeance and the desire to right the wrong. The champion of the cause was Pope Eugenius III; but the man who really put the armies on the road to the Orient was the great spiritual leader of the period, Bernard of Clairvaux. Answering his call, armies gathered in France and Germany, this time led by their kings: Louis VII and Konrad III. In 1148 the Second Crusade reached the Holy Land. Everyone expected the European knighthood and the Crusader armies to attack and recapture Edessa, capital and county. And indeed, such an attack, launched from Antioch, might have stemmed the tide of the ascending Nur el-Din.

What actually happened was the worst thing imaginable. The European monarchs and crusaders decided to attack . . . Damascus! This step seems so improbable that historians are still discussing what could have brought the armies of the Second Crusade to the walls of this city. At that point events became even more confused, as the besieging armies – after initial success – were shamefully forced to retire after four days of fighting. The European leaders openly accused the cru-

saders of taking Damascene bribes to bring about the failure of the siege.
The Second Crusade was over. Edessa remained Moslem and the
political bungling of the crusade literally pushed Damascus (1154)
into the willing arms of Nur el-Din. The loss of face and the failure
of the crusade were aggravated by the storm of European criticism,
which effectively prevented the launching of a new crusade despite
efforts of Bernard of Clairvaux and Suger of St Denis.

In the Moslem north the crusaders now faced a power far more
consolidated than ever before. This brought them into closer relations
with Byzantium, which until now had appeared more often as rival
than ally. Both sides were ready to compromise. The crusaders even
acknowledged Byzantine suzerainty over Antioch and for a short time
accepted a Greek patriarch in the city. Emperor Manuel I Comnenus
restored and embellished ecclesiastical buildings in the kingdom,
and Greek monasteries were not the only ones restored. The nave
and transept of the Church of the Nativity in Bethlehem were covered
with resplendent, scintillating mosaics, and the interior of the Church
of the Holy Sepulchre also enjoyed his bounty. Inscriptions in Greek
and Latin seemed to usher in an oecumenical spirit of alliance between
the most Orthodox and the most Catholic kingdoms.

The solid Moslem front in the north compelled the Franks to look
southwards. The hour was propitious, for Egypt was the sick man
on the Nile. The once strong Fatimid caliphate retained merely a
shadow of its former power. The viziers who ruled the country changed
in an accelerating rhythm of revolts and advancement by assassination.
The advance of the Crusader frontier in 1150 to Gaza, which lay on the
fringe of the desert, already pointed to Egypt, as did an attack on el-
Arish in 1161, after which Egypt paid a yearly tribute to the crusaders. Finally, an occasion to intervene arose in 1163, when one
of the two contending viziers in Cairo turned to Amalric, king of
Jerusalem, for help. During the next six years, the crusaders invaded
Egypt five times. There was a fairly good chance that Egypt, like
Damascus some years earlier, would cease to be a danger. If the crusaders' southern neighbour could not be an ally, a neutralised Egypt
could at least counter-balance the threat in the north. Moreover,
Byzantium was ready to cooperate with the crusaders, and its fleet
was ready to move into Egypt. But the Christian alliance was short-
lived, as the Crusaders were sure they could win a victory by themselves and share the spoils with no one.

Crusader intervention on behalf of one of the contending viziers caused the other Egyptian faction to look for a protector, and diplomat missions were hastily despatched to Nur el-Din. The latter was un-unwilling to intervene, but finally his lieutenant Shirkuh, a Kurdish commander leading Syrian and Mesopotamian contingents, by-passed the Crusader fortresses in Transjordan and made his way to Egypt. The crusaders and Syrian Moslems fought their battles on Egyptian soil. Almost all the battles ended in Crusader victories, but no expedition was ultimately successful. Crusader flags fluttered over Cairo and were seen below the walls of Alexandria, but the whole Egyptian episode ended in a fiasco. The crusaders overplayed their hand. Their monetary demands grew, and at one point they even considered annexing Egypt. This, however, was too much for the Egyptian masses. While the fight for power took place among generals, and did not affect the population, the Christian presence did. Shirkuh found increasing popular support, and the crusaders were forced to retire. The dream of ruling Egypt remained an enticing mirage.

These hazardous expeditions not only strained the military and financial resources of the Latin kingdom, but their failure changed the map of the Middle East. Shirkuh became vizier of Egypt and upon his death (1169) he was succeeded by his nephew, the famous Saladin. Two years later, at the death of the caliph, the Fatimid caliphate became extinct (1171), and the Abbaside caliph of Baghdad was nominally acknowledged in Egypt. Contrary to expectations, Egypt and Syria did not unite against the crusaders. During Nur el-Din's last years (he died in 1174), tension escalated between the Syrian ruler and Saladin, his official lieutenant in Egypt. Cooperation between Egypt and Syria against the crusaders had to wait for Syria and Mesopotamia to be subjugated by the Egyptian army led by Saladin.

Saladin the Kurd, the great hero of Moslem history, was first and foremost a leader of men. A rather mediocre general, he was a gifted statesman, generous to friend and foe, unselfish and a source of con-fidence. In the eyes of the great masses of Islam, he represented the embodiment of Moslem virtues, the ideal leader for the Holy War against the Infidel. Yet before attacking the Crusader kingdom, and after a painful defeat at the battle of Montgisart in 1177, Saladin began the conquest of Moslem Syria, ruled by the descendents of his bene-factor, Nur el-Din. Damascus was easily taken (1174), but it took almost ten years before Zengid Syria recognised the new ruler. It was Aleppo, supported by the crusaders of Antioch, which held out longest, until 1183. Only then, with his power consolidated did Saladin begin preparations for an all-out effort against the crusaders.

Together with the opposition in Egypt the crusaders tried unsuccessfully to conspire against Saladin. A number of daring raids across Sinai brought them to the vicinity of the lakes of Suez, while others went to Taima in northern Hejaz. But the most daring expedition was that organised by Renaud of Châtillon. The former prince consort of Antioch, a prisoner of war for some seventeen years, was now the prince consort of the Lady Eschive of Transjordan. There he conceived a daring plan to penetrate the Red Sea and possibly to raid Mecca and Medina, though his ultimate aim was probably to control the international traffic between Asia and Egypt through Bab el-Mandeb. In 1182 a fleet constructed in the desert castle of Crac was transported piecemeal about 125 miles over the desert road to the Bay of 'Aqaba, where it was put together and launched into the Red Sea. Jazirat Far'un, the little island facing 'Aqaba, was captured and a meandering razzia ensued, during which the crusaders looted and sacked ports in Egypt and Hejaz. It took weeks before dumbfounded Egypt reacted, and when its fleet finally located the crusaders, led by Bedouins, in the Hejaz desert, they were only a short distance from Medina!

During the time a Crusader baron was conducting his own foreign policy, the kingdom was weakened by internal dissension. Raymond of Tripoli, representing the native Crusader nobility, and Guy of Lusignan, a relative newcomer who had ascended to the throne of Jerusalem as the husband of its heiress Sybille, tore the kingdom apart. Opposed by the native aristocracy, the gallant and courageous (but not too wise) king of Jerusalem hardly had time to impose his authority before Saladin struck through the Golan Heights at Tiberias, the capital of Galilee. Despite dissension the crusaders rallied around their king, but, instead of waiting in excellent strategic position in Galilee, they followed poor advice and moved towards the Sea of Galilee to rescue the besieged city. On a scorching summer day, 4 July 1187, they were trapped on a small plain closed in by the Horns of Hittin. The whole Crusader army, some 1,200 knights (including the Military Orders) and some 20,000 foot soldiers, was massacred or taken captive. They represented all the kingdom's available strength. What followed the defeat at Hittin was more like a military parade than a campaign. City after city and castle after castle opened their gates when summoned by Saladin, who granted them free exit to what was left of Christian territory. On 2 October 1187, after eighty-eight years of Christian domination, Jerusalem opened its gates to Saladin. A few months later only Tyre in the Latin kingdom, Antioch and Tripoli in the north and a few scattered castles remained in Christian hands. It seemed that the last hour of the kingdom had struck.

Then Europe reacted. The loss of Jerusalem was not only a loss of a capital and what it stood for; it was the loss of the most tangible symbol of faith – the Holy Sepulchre. The Lord's tomb was again captive in the hands of the Infidel. A great new crusade was preached all over the West. The lead was assumed by the crowned heads of Western Christendom. Almost seventy, Emperor Frederick I Barbarossa led contigents from Germany; Richard the Lionhearted of England led Anglo-Norman and Aquitanian knighthood; Philip II Augustus, the great Capetian state builder, led the forces of France; and members of the highest European nobility moved on the East. It took almost two years before the Crusade, or rather parts of it, reached the shores of the Holy Land by different routes. The German expedition, which took the over-land route, secured its way through agreements with the rulers of Hungary and Byzantium. This largest of the contingents suffered heavy losses in crossing Asia Minor, but its most painful loss was the death of the old emperor, who drowned in the Calycadnus River in Lesser Armenia before entering northern Syria. The morale of the German army was undermined, making it difficult for the duke of Swabia to bring the remnants of the host to the Holy Land. Richard I and Philip II took different sea routes but met in Sicily, where they passed the winter of 1190/1. Here they became embroiled in local struggles and exchanged rivalries of their own, officially put aside on the eve of the common crusade to the Mediterranean island. They both set sail in 1191, but Richard arrived second, as on the way to Acre he captured the island of Cyprus from its Byzantine governor.

The two and a half years which had elapsed between the fall of Jerusalem and the arrival of the contingents of the Third Crusade might have annihilated any prospect of restoration had it not been for Conrad of Montferrat, who – sailing from Constantinople – miraculously escaped being taken prisoner in Moslem Acre and put into the port of Tyre. There, in the only city still in Christian hands, he found those who had escaped Saladin's sword, as well as those whom the Moslem leader had allowed to retire to Christian territory as the price of capitulation. The city was without a leader. Conrad immediately reorganised the defence of the city and valiantly withstood Saladin's threats and siege. At the same time, Guy of Lusignan, the unfortunate king of Jerusalem who had been taken prisoner at Hittin but had been released on parole, broke his oath to Saladin and began to assemble the meagre remnants of the Crusader forces. The gates of Tyre were shut in his face on Montferrat's orders, but his small contingent courageously moved to the plain of Acre and took up positions facing the city (1189). Thus Tyre and the Bay of Acre became the bridgeheads of the Third Crusade.

With the arrival of the duke of Swabia in the autumn of 1190, the Crusader armies began to grow; and the arrival of the French in spring 1191, followed by the Anglo-Normans two months later, swelled their numbers. Beleaguered Acre, by now under Crusader siege for two years, became the focus of European and Near Eastern history. The city was blocked from the sea and encircled on land by crusaders, who in turn were besieged by the armies of Saladin camped in a huge semicircle from shore to shore. Despite Saladin's efforts to get new forces and provisions into the beleaguered city, its defenders could withstand the Crusader onslaughts no longer. The city capitulated in July 1191, and Acre became the first victory of the Third Crusade *reconquista*. Unfortunately, the conquest of the city was immediately followed by the departure of the greater part of the army for home. Of the leaders, only Richard remained for an entire year, achieving a splendid victory over Saladin in the battle of Arsuf and recuperating maritime cities as far south as Jaffa. His efforts to lay siege to Jerusalem brought him within a few miles of the city, but the capital itself was not captured.

The tremendous expenditure of human life and money which accompanied the crusade was now painfully felt in both camps. Pressed by the news from England, Richard could not stay on in the Holy Land indefinitely. Likewise, Saladin's resources and manpower were dwindling, and his heterogeneous Syrian and Egyptian contingents resented every extension of their stay in the field. Accordingly, in September 1192 the two sides signed a peace treaty which fixed frontiers roughly according to the existing status quo. The second kingdom of Jerusalem was born as a narrow strip of land precariously clinging to the seaboard from Beirut to Jaffa. Jerusalem, the goal of the crusade, remained Moslem, and the only area where some breadth

Oꝛ estoit a graunt merueille la cite de
sur ⸱ ꞇ moult enciēne ⸱ S̄ pins qui mot
fut decloꝛs isuttez ⸱ si com len dit ⸱ li roumein ⸱

The conquest of the ports was vital to maintain communications with Europe.
This 13th-century illumination shows Tyre blockaded by the Venetian
fleet and besieged by Crusader knighthood (13)

Crac de Moab, a 12th-century fortress built on the marches of the Crusader
kingdom in Transjordan, was one of the fortifications built to guard the
desert frontier (14)

The Crusader challenge resurrected the Moslem idea of the *jihad* in the Moslem academies. A library from a 13th-century manuscript of al-Hariri's *Maqamat* (15)

Nur el-Din built a marvellous preacher's chair in Aleppo, and Saladin placed it in al-Aqsa after his conquest of Jerusalem (16)

The Great Mosque of Damascus, the capital of Moslem Syria and the centre of Islamic culture (17)

above The Horns of Hittin, where the crusaders lost a battle (July 1187) and a kingdom (18)

above The seal of Richard the Lionhearted, king of England. Reality and legend combined to make him the hero of a nation and of Christendom (19)

above The last great crusade was led by Louis IX of France (St Louis), and his flagship carried the royal family to the East. From an illuminated biography of St Louis by Guillaume de St Pathus (20)

left The Isle de Graye (Jezirat Far'un), a Crusader outpost on the Red Sea where Renaud of Châtillon launched a daring razzia against Mecca and attempted to reach the Indian Ocean (21)

After the fall of Acre (1291) and the end of the Latin kingdom of Jerusalem, the crown of Jerusalem passed to the Lusignans of Cyprus, whose kingdom existed for another two hundred years. This was the heraldic emblem of the Lusignans, the kings of Cyprus and nominal kings of Jerusalem (22)

was given to the kingdom was between Jaffa and Ramle, along the main road to the unattainable Holy City.

The great expectations of the Third Crusade gave way to despair and an acid indictment of its leadership. Two years of effort by almost all the nations of Europe were compared with the meagre achievements of the expeditions. Then, vindictive criticism gave way to a more sober analysis, and some began to ask whether the Crusades were divinely inspired. Despite the ideological crisis, smaller expeditions were organised at the end of the twelfth century to bolster the position of the kingdom. They tried, not unsuccessfully, to enlarge the Christian hold in the East, and among their other conquests they added Beirut to the kingdom. Objectively, the situation again seemed propitious. The death of Saladin in 1195 resulted in an almost immediate disintegration of his empire. It was the man and not an inherent principle or inner cohesion which had kept it together. The scions of the house of Ayyub in Syria, Mesopotamia and distant Yemen, while theoretically acknowledging the suzerainty of the ruler of Cairo, actually pursued independent policies, and old jealousies and rivalries disrupted the painfully achieved unity. It was in these circumstances that Europe, constantly exhorted by the crusaders and the papacy, began to arm for a new expedition, the ill-famed Fourth Crusade.

The vicissitudes of the Fourth Crusade from beginning to dramatic end are shrouded in a dense fog of uncertainties. The spiritual father of the expedition was the most magnificent of medieval popes, Innocent III; its leaders were the great ruling houses of Europe – Theobald of Champagne, Baldwin of Flanders, Philip of Swabia, Boniface of Montferrat; its aim – a direct attack on Egypt. By 1201, after several years of preparation, the Crusade was gathering in the port of Venice; but a year later it was besieging . . . Christian Constantinople! The accusations and counter-accusations which began immediately after the capture of the Byzantine capital continue to our time. Though now deprived of an axe to grind, historians lay the blame for the diversion of the Crusade alternately on the German Guelfs, the greed of the northern barons, a Byzantine pretender and above all Venice.

The main events are clear, but the motives behind them leave the problem of responsibility unsolved. The Crusade was planned via the sea route to evade the difficulties encountered by earlier expeditions in crossing Asia Minor. Transportation had to be effected by a Venetian fleet specially mobilised or built by the republic and paid for by the

crusaders. When the various contingents of the Crusader host con-
verged on Venice in the autumn of 1201, it became clear that the transport expenses could not be met. The Venetians nevertheless maintained
the offer of their services, but for a different kind of remuneration:
the capture of the Hungarian city of Zara on the Adriatic Sea (a thorn
in the side of Venice, the queen of the Adriatic). The crusaders agreed,
and Zara – a Christian city of a Christian kingdom – was captured.
This move was followed by an even more fateful decision. Some
years earlier Isaac II Angelus, emperor of Byzantium, had been dethroned by Alexius III. Isaac's son, Alexius IV Angelus, who tried to
get help from the German court, appeared before the Crusader host
at Zara and convinced them to attack Constantinople and restore
him to power. The restoration, he promised, would make Byzantine
resources available for the Crusade, in addition to a bountiful remuneration to the liberating host. Venice viewed the idea as a major opportunity to implant herself in Byzantium and thus dominate one of the
greatest commercial centres of the world. The Byzantine pretender
also found support among the Germans, as his wife, Irene, was the sister
of Philip of Swabia. Still, despite so many vested interests, the under-
taking against Constantinople would have been impossible had it not
been for the persistent latent antagonism between the West and Byzantium. The mutual resentment smoldered during the First Crusade, then
flared into open animosity during the Third Crusade, when Byzantium
was openly charged, and not unreasonably, of connivance with Saladin.

Though the idea might initially have been to force Byzantium into
an alliance to aid the Crusader kingdom, the expedition itself altered
the aim. The landing of the crusaders in Constantinople routed the
usurper, and Alexius IV Angelus, the Crusader protégé, became the
ruler of the empire (July 1203). But when the promised renumeration
was not forthcoming, the crusaders stormed the city (April 1204).
Baldwin of Flanders became the first emperor of the new state, the
Latin Empire of Constantinople; a Venetian became its first Latin
patriarch; and the empire was divided, as are so many spoils, among
the victors. Venice, now ruler of 'a quarter and a half' of the empire,
established its own maritime empire in the islands of the Aegean.

A Crusader establishment now existed at Constantinople, and the
Lusignans ruled the independent kingdom of Cyprus, which acknowledged the suzerainty of the Roman Empire, as did Lesser Armenia
(whose ruler received his crown from the emperor's envoys). Theo-

retically, all these kingdoms could have served as bases to bolster the precarious Latin kingdom of Jerusalem. In practice, however, things were otherwise. Each kingdom had its own problems; Europe was scandalized by the attack on a Christian empire; and those still willing to migrate preferred Cyprus and Constantinople, much richer and far less dangerous than the Crusader establishment in the Holy Land.

In the meanwhile, the Latin kingdom enjoyed almost a decade of peace, partially due to the tensions in the Ayyubi camp which ruled Egypt. The respite was a blessing, as it was clear that the forces of the kingdom were no match for the Moslems. The kingdom's hope was in a new great Crusade, which grew more and more difficult to organise.

Still, despite obvious setbacks, the idea of the crusade was not abandoned. Undaunted by the last fiasco, Innocent III urged a new expedition. Criticism and resentment notwithstanding, here and there a messianic spark still glowed, as witnessed by one of the most curious medieval phenomena, the Children's Crusade of 1212. Led by two young boys, one from Germany and the other from France, the bands of adolescents crossed their countries to the shores of the Mediterranean believing they would find a dry passage to the Holy Land, like that of Israel of old across the Red Sea. The movement was nourished on the belief that what Providence would not grant to adults, sinners by definition, it would grant to children, symbols of innocence. But, the children found their way into the lands of Islam under the decks of Christian slave-ships and were sold in North Africa.

The crusade preached by Innocent III, proclaimed in 1215 at the Fourth Lateran Council, finally got under way two years after the great pontiff's death (1217). This posthumous crusade of Innocent III, often known as the Fifth Crusade, opens a new chapter in crusader history. Its most salient characteristic was its aim: Egypt. There were many reasons to prompt the landing in the Nile delta rather than near the Jordan River, but two seem to be dominant: the particular interest of the Italian commercial cities in dominating the central mart of the Mediterranean, and the new political and military doctrine of the crusaders. It was not the first time that the crusaders had intended to attack Egypt. But whereas the twelfth-century expeditions of King Amalric intended to make Egypt a tributary or even a possession of the Latin kingdom, the Fifth Crusade intended to win back on the battle-fields of Egypt the Crusader kingdom lost at the Horns of Hittin.

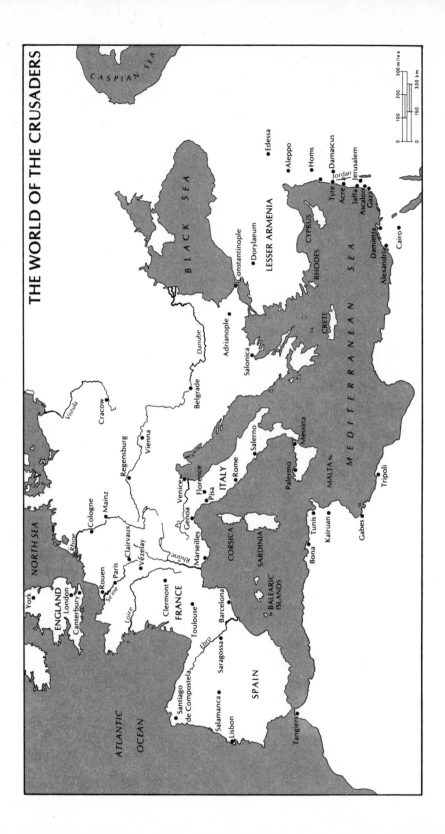

THE WORLD OF THE CRUSADERS

CASPIAN SEA

BLACK SEA

ATLANTIC OCEAN

NORTH SEA

York
ENGLAND
London
Canterbury

Rouen
Paris
Seine
Loire
Clermont
FRANCE
Vézelay
Clairvaux
Rhône
Marseilles

Santiago de Compostela
Saragossa
Salamanca
Lisbon
SPAIN
Barcelona
Ebro
Tangiers

Cologne
Mainz
Rhine
Regensburg
Vienna
Cracow
Vistula

BALEARIC ISLANDS

CORSICA
SARDINIA
Po
Venice
Florence
Pisa
Genoa
ITALY
Rome
Salerno
Messina
Palermo
MALTA

Bona
Tunis
Kairuan
Gabes
Tripoli

Belgrade
Danube
Adrianople
Salonica

Constantinople
Dorylaeum

LESSER ARMENIA

CRETE
RHODES
CYPRUS

MEDITERRANEAN SEA

Edessa
Aleppo
Homs
Damascus
Jordan
Tyre
Acre
Jaffa
Jerusalem
Ascalon
Gaza
Damietta
Alexandria
Cairo

300 miles
300 km
100 200
0 150 300

One of the most remarkable results of the Third Crusade was the 'scorched-earth policy' initiated by Saladin and later followed by his Damascene successors. Saladin had rightly understood the importance of fortifications, city and castle, in the Crusader hold on the Holy Land. Not only the security of the kingdom, but the very ability to rule the country in times of peace depended upon fortifications. Effective Crusader rule extended only as far as direct supervision, centred in Crusader fortifications. Should these strongholds disappear, there would be no way to re-establish Crusader rule save by wholesale restoration, meaning a tremendous outlay of money and a great supply of manpower. Moreover, after the Third Crusade, as long as the kingdom's territory almost coincided with the narrow coastal plain, any such effort could be nipped in the bud by the neighbouring Moslem garrisons. Consequently, Saladin embarked on a policy of systematically destroying almost all the Crusader castles and city fortifications which fell into his hands. The peace treaty with Richard the Lionhearted even stipulated the destruction of several Crusader strongholds. The destruction was thorough, and what was not done by Saladin was accomplished by the ruler of Damascus.

The crusaders drew the logical conclusion. The impossibility of a wholesale restoration was obvious. There was not enough money, manpower and, above all, enthusiasm to start the conquest all over again in conditions far more difficult than those of a hundred years years earlier. The result was to direct the crusade to Egypt. A great victory, so went the reasoning, would bring Egypt to its knees and force it into a peace settlement which would stipulate the cession of the kingdom in its old boundaries. Controlling Egypt, which would withdraw its garrisons from the Holy Land, the kingdom could be restored and refortified by the united effort of Christendom, financed by indemnities from Egypt.

This was the plan of the Fifth Crusade, which all in all lasted some four years. In more than one sense it was a German crusade in which the duke of Austria and the King of Hungary also participated. Gathering in Acre from 1217, the Crusader fleet landed and besieged Damietta in 1218. The leader of the host was John of Brienne (King of Jerusalem by marriage), but during the siege the papal legate, Cardinal Pelagius, took command. In 1219 Damietta was taken, but it was the new command which now dictated the terms. The year-long stay in captured Damietta, to divide spoils but also to wait for the frequently postponed arrival of Emperor Frederick II, proved fatal to the expedition. When the host finally did move towards Cairo, it found itself before the newly erected fortification later called Mansura, where the sultan repeated his offer of peace: restoration of the kingdom (excluding Transjordan) and payment of indemnities against the evacuation of Egypt. The terms were generous, but despite John of Brienne's acceptance, they were rejected by Pelagius. War was inevitable. The Moslem army, which in the meantime had received Syrian reinforcements, cut off the crusaders off from their rear in Damietta and stopped their march southwards on Cairo. Trapped, the crusaders had to evacuate Egypt as the price of freedom. The crusade was over and the new fiasco added to the general disappointment and accusations of irresponsibility. The Crusades were quickly becoming an object of ridicule in European public opinion. Their only tangible results were the fortification of some cities and castles in the kingdom – among them the huge Pilgrim's Castle of the Templars and Montfort of the Teutonic Order, begun by the Fifth Crusade before its move on Egypt.

Nonetheless, a new crusade was gathering. Emperor Frederick II, who had taken crusading vows as early as 1215 but postponed the expedition year after year, alleging difficulties in his kingdom of Sicily, in the empire and with his health, finally embarked in the summer of 1228. His crusading vows, position of emperor in Christendom and not least his title as king of Jerusalem through marriage with Isabella (daughter of John of Brienne), heiress of the kingdom, made the crusade imperative. Political circumstances made it the strangest of all crusades. Pope Gregory IX, enraged by Frederick's apparent procrastination and tergiversation, anathemised the emperor. This was only the first act of a strange spectacle: the excommunicated lay head of Christendom leading a crusade. Stranger things followed. Frederick II, who was more Sicilian than anything else and to whom Islam was not a closed book and Moslems more than a race of Infidels to be exterminated, began talks with el-Malik al-Kamil, ruler of Egypt. Playing to the best the sultan's difficulties at home and with his Syrian relations, Frederick II, whose small contingent drew ridicule from his opponents and embittered his friends, succeeded in bringing the sultan to a most favourable agreement in February 1299. First and foremost, Jerusalem was ceded to the crusaders, though without the Temple esplanade and its mosques, as was Bethlehem and Nazareth. Two corridors, from Jaffa via Ramle to Jerusalem and from Acre through Galilee to Nazareth, became Christian. One would expect that in the face of such tremendous success, old quarrels would be patched up or buried; but just the opposite was true. The success enraged the pope even more, and the anathemised emperor's ride to Jerusalem was organised so that crusader and military orders' contingents should not need to be in contact with him. When the emperor finally entered the city, the bells of Jerusalem were silenced as the Holy City was laid under interdict.

The emperor entered the Church of the Holy Sepulchre, took the crown of Jerusalem from the altar and placed it on his own head. Only the faithful Teutonic knights participated; but despite anathema and interdict, the crusaders from the Holy Land and those from overseas could not contain their joy at being in liberated Jerusalem.

Frederick II's return to Europe was condemned by the opposition as abandoning the kingdom, which would be unable to defend its new acquisitions. Although the pope lifted the ban from the emperor (it was imposed again some years later), the kingdom itself was dismembered by the war between the emperor's representatives in the East and the native Crusader aristocracy. Imperial strongholds in Cyprus and the kingdom were captured after ten years of internal struggle. The creation of a ruling revolutionary commune resulted in feudal oligarchy. The Crusader kingdom was disintegrating.

It was the crusaders' good luck that neighbouring Islam fared no better. Damascus became the focus of opposition to Egypt, the emirate of Transjordan was in the process of changing allies and all three were willing to accept the crusaders as allies. Unfortunately, the Latin kingdom lacked a leader. Templars and Hospitallers were divided, one supporting a Damascene alliance, the other an Egyptian one. The crusade of Theobald of Champagne (1239–40) followed by that of Richard of Cornwall (1240–1), succeeded, by playing up the division in the Moslem camp, in enlarging the boundaries of the kingdom significantly by annexing Galilee. There were some attempts to fortify the kingdom, marked by the erection of the Templars' fortress in Safed and the fortification of Ascalon. But new dangers from within and without soon annihilated the earlier diplomatic successes.

The tensions and wars among Egypt, Damascus, Transjordan and the Crusader kingdom in the confined fertile band around the eastern Mediterranean, important as they were for the participants, seem like insignificant quibbling when compared with the tremendous upheaval which changed the face of Asia and for generations determined the fate of Eastern Europe. In distant Qaraqorum in Central Asia, a new star was rising, that of the ruler of all the Mongols, Genghis Khan. Having mastered the Mongolian tribes, the new power expanded with the speed of its small, sturdy horses, and in less than a generation it over-ran China in the east and, moving like a deadly avalanche which destroys everything in its path, subjugated the Russian steppes in the west until checked in 1241 on the Polish-German frontier, whereas in the south Persia and Mesopotamia fell to the conquerors. A Euro-Asian empire larger than any until then known in history was founded on the smoul-dering ruins of earlier civilisations. The waves of Mongolian conquest were moving to the shores of the Mediterranean, and the Crusader states were on the fringes of that empire.

The rumble of Mongolian hoofs was nearing when the crusaders joined in a Damascene alliance against Egypt. Threatened by the apparently strong coalition, Egypt invoked the aid of the Khwarizmi-ans, a nation dislodged by the Mongolian invasion from its ancestral lands near the Caspian Sea and turned into wandering mercenaries in the Near East. Egyptians and Khwarizmians inflicted upon the crusaders, deserted at the last minute by the Damascenes, a costly defeat in the battle of Gaza. Immediately afterwards, the Khwarizmians overran Jerusalem (1244), and the Holy City ceased to be Christian, and only seven hundred years later did it witness a Christian army, the British under Allenby, taking over the city from the Ottoman Turks.

The approaching danger of the Mongols stirred Europe to seek out new allies. Ever since 1245, when Pope Innocent IV sent Giovanni of Piano Carpini to the Mongolian court – followed by St Louis's emissary, William of Rubruquis (1248–9) – persistent rumours had circulated about Christians among the Mongolian tribes. This was partially true, as Nestorian propaganda in Central Asia had converted some Mongols, albeit only a small minority, to Christianity. The loss of Jerusalem and the Mongolian threat prompted a new crusade, the last great crusade, that of St Louis, the king of France. The concentra-tion point of the new crusade was Cyprus, plentifully supplied for the expedition. From here, in the spring of 1249, the host sailed for Egypt. Damietta was captured again and the army moved towards Cairo, but, like the Fifth Crusade, it was trapped at Mansura, where a daring but

opposite The capture of Baghdad by the Mongols in 1258, from an illuminated Persian manuscript

entirely superfluous sortie of the king's brother ended in disaster. The king and the entire Christian army were captured. In return for their release, the crusaders had to evacuate Egypt and pay a crushing ransom of almost one million gold pieces.

The crusade was over. Those who returned (May 1250) to stay on in Acre spent the next four years fortifying or strengthening the fortifications of the Crusader cities on the shore. Sidon, Acre, Caesarea and Jaffa added bastion, tower and wall to the existing ones. But Europe turned a deaf ear to entreaties for help. Only a new movement of adolescents, called the Pastoreaux, moved southwards. As its slogan was the crusade and it simultaneously attacked the clergy, it was quickly brought to a halt by lay and ecclesiastical authorities alike.

The fortifications along the coast assured the existence of the kingdom for some time, though their logic was based on the premise that a new crusade would be organised to aid the Holy Land. In the meantime, two events changed the whole framework of the Near East. During the crusade of St Louis, a revolution which broke out in Egypt (1249) dethroned the Ayyubid dynasty founded by Saladin and brought to power the military caste of the Mameluks, thus instituting one of the most curious régimes in history. The Mameluks, not unlike the later Ottoman Janissaries, were slaves, predominantly bought by the Black Sea, converted to Islam and raised as professional warriors. Only one bought as a slave could enter their ranks, but once in the Mameluk regiments one could reach the highest positions in state and army.

In 1260 the man who ruled Egypt was the Mameluk Baybars, a brilliant general and excellent administrator. Thorough and ruthless, Baybars was one of the greatest rulers of Islam, and in more than one sense he changed the destinies of the Near East. The financial resources of Egypt were strongly taken in hand and the last idling Ayyubids were replaced by energetic, self-made men. The Egyptian revolution deepened the gap between Cairo and Syria, which was still ruled by the epigones of the Ayyubid dynasty. A confrontation was approaching when the Mongolian flood reached Iraq. Baghdad was captured by Mongolian hordes in 1258. To prevent a cosmic catastrophe if the holy blood of the caliph would be spilled, the thirty-eighth and last Abbaside caliph was put into a sack and strangled to death. The Mongolian armies commanded by Hulagu took Damascus. War with Egypt was imminent. In the great confrontation, the crusaders, lacking leadership and weakened from within by a fratricidal war between the Italian communes, remained helpless onlookers, though the decisive battle of Ain Jalut (1260) was fought at their doorstep (at the place where Gideon had fought the Midianites, (Ein Harod). The Mongols suffered a heavy defeat and quickly receded towards Syria. It was one of the crucial battles in history as it decided that the Near East would remain Moslem and not Mongolian. Later, Baybars was victorious again, pushing the Mongols back to Persia and Armenia.

By pursuing the retreating Mongols, Baybars became master of Moslem Syria, thus encircling the remnants of the Crusader kingdom on all sides. It would have been easy to attack and destroy it, but Baybars had more pressing occupations. Despite his victories, the Mongols presented a real danger. Baybars again launched the slogan of the *jihad*, this time against the Mongols, and tried to create a Moslem coalition which was also to include the Golden Horde, the Mongol state on the shores of the Black Sea.

Three short campaigns (1263–6) deprived the crusaders of Safed and other castles in Galilee. Caesarea was lost, as well as Arsuf. The narrow band of the kingdom became shorter, and the Crusader cities on the coast were now isolated from one another by Moslem territory. For a moment it seemed that a new crusade would still be able to use the Crusader bridgeheads and begin a *reconquista*. And actually a great crusade was launched by St Louis, but it went to Tunis, whose ruler was allegedly ready to accept Christianity. The dying king reportedly whispered: Jerusalem, Jerusalem. But the idea of the crusade was by now almost extinct. Attempts by James of Aragon (who only got half way to the Holy Land) and Edward I of England were more part of a code of chivalry than crusades which could really change the situation. Still, they were enough to deter Baybars and his successors, who were obsessed by the idea of a new crusade. As the Crusader cities did not bother the Mameluk rulers, the latter were ready to grant them truces, which could be broken at an opportune moment.

The crown of Jerusalem was handed over to the Lusignans of Cyprus, but even their sincerest efforts could not change the situation. The establishments were disappearing piece by piece. Antioch was captured in 1286 and Tripoli in 1289. Finally the great Crusader bulwark, Acre, was captured after a valiant forty-four day siege on 18 May 1291. This was the end. In August 1291 the Templars abandoned the greatest of Crusader fortifications, the Pilgrim's Castle. This sealed the fate of the great European pilgrimage and marked the end of the kingdom.

4

The Levant

It was somewhere between Italy and the Balkans that the armed masses of the First Crusade made their first contact with the East. This was still Christendom: the Christian Orient, the eastern half of the ancient Roman Empire, Byzantium. The road through the Balkans, Constantinople and parts of Asia Minor was the prelude to the Orient at large, the Orient of Islam, now entrenched not far from the walls of the Byzantine capital. From here it extended through Mesopotamia, Syria and the Holy Land to India in the East, Egypt and the whole of North Africa in the West.

For the Westerner, from England, France or Germany, both faces of the Orient – Christian and Moslem – were uncharted land. Greek, Syriac, Arabic – un-Christian languages – were spoken by Christians. Magnificent but strange churches and monasteries, cities of classical fame (or what was left of them), a non-Latin liturgy celebrated with pomp, dresses worth a prince's ransom on the oriental clergy, incense and perfumes, all this was the fabulous Orient, scintillating, perfume-laden, luxurious, the nearest one could approach the earthly paradise. Italians and the Normans of southern Italy were not entirely strangers to the East. The former trafficked with Constantinople and the Moslem Levant; the latter was acquainted with it through invasions carried out before the First Crusade into the Byzantine Balkans. And then there was Venice, an oriental city floating on its canals and seas under Christian banners, the Orient's outlet to the West, the European check-point before slipping into the exotic East.

For two hundred years Westerners lived surrounded by the Orient and Orientals: Moslems, Arab and Persian aristocracy, the nomadic Bedouin roaming from the Euphrates to the Nile, the Turkish commanders and their garrisons, sectarian Druze and the fear-inspiring sect of the Assassins, the fellaheen of Syria and Palestine and the peasants of the Nile valley. All bowed to one of the two great Moslem centers, the fabulous Sunnite court of the caliph of Baghdad or the no-less fabulous Shi'ite caliph of Cairo. There were also the oriental Christians, whom one went to save from the Moslem yoke but somehow never came to like, let alone understand. Their ruler was the mighty Byzantine emperor enthroned on the Bosporus. The Westerner was dazzled and confused by his palaces, the bejewelled crowns, the pearl-spangled dresses, the gold-woven materials, the hieratic behaviour of state officers, the strange army with Greeks, Slavs and Vikings from the far north rubbing shoulders with Turkish warriors who served as bodyguards and police officers. Then there was the Greek Orthodox Church and its own patriarchs who obstinately refused to recognise the supremacy of the papal see in Rome. Its clergy was proud of thousand-year-old traditions, claiming them to be more authentic than those of the West; its patriarch and bishops resided not only within the boundaries of the Christian empire, but also in Moslem lands, where they were accepted and often honoured by the Moslems. One could hardly understand this strange situation, but one was offended by the Greek insistence on functioning autonomously in the lands newly liberated from the Moslems and now under the rule of the Latin Crusaders.

The Orient also contained Christian kingdoms, albeit not orthodox; but being far away from home one was more lenient and even proud and comforted to know that they existed. Far in the north, in the Caucasus Mountains, lay the Christian kingdom of Georgia (Grusia), which was sometimes called Iberia. With its own king, princes and army, it played a role in the politics of Asia Minor. Its population and clergy had their own language and alphabet, their relations with the Holy Land were age-long and their clergymen and emissaries were often to be found in the courts of the Moslem, Turkish, Persian and later Mongolian potentates. Further on was the kingdom of Lesser Armenia in the Taurus Mountains and along the coastal plain of Cilicia in Asia Minor. In direct contact with the principality of Antioch, it later influenced and was in turn influenced by the Franks. Its rulers, famous for their military valour, cultivated a kind of provincial Byzantine court. Its fighters were famous, and Armenia often supplied converted viziers to the Moslem courts and mercenaries to the potentates of the Moslem and Christian Orient. The peculiar garb of its clergy and monks and Armenian crosses with their split branches, as well as the unique architecture of their sanctuaries, their doctors and miniature painters were quite familiar to the crusaders. After two generations of coexistence, intermarriage with the Franks made the French language and customs a dominant factor of Armenian court life.

These real Christian kingdoms on the frontiers of Islam were probably less famous than the legendary Christian empire of the Presbyter John. Located alternately in fabulous India or no-less exotic Ethiopia, it was often a ray of hope when Moslem danger menaced and one counted the multitudes of Moslem adversaries. What was certainly not legend, however, was the existence of a Christian kingdom in Ethiopia. Ecclesiastically tied to the Coptic patriarch of Alexandria, the Abyssinian monks and their monasteries, which evoked images of the earliest monastic establishments in Christendom, added to the heterogeneity of the Orient. Their closest neighbours were the Moslems of Egypt, but the Christian Copts of Egypt had strong links with the kingdom whose dynasty claimed to be the offspring of King Solomon and the Queen of Sheba.

The Orient, Moslem and Christian alike, was the great discovery of the Crusades. Naturally it was known to exist, for pilgrims, merchants and mercenaries had visited there. But with the Crusades the Orient became an integral part of the European *imago mundi*, the picture of the inhabited world; and this was a major development in the expanding Western consciousness of lands, peoples and cultures beyond Europe. The various oriental elements all played a role in the life of the Crusader colonies in the East. Islam was met not only on the footing of war but also on the level of economic relations, as its followers made up the majority of population that lived in the crusader-dominated areas.

Some of the Moslems on the coasts of the Levant were descendants of the seventh-century Arab conquerors who annihilated the Byzantine domination of Syria, Palestine and Egypt. But the majority of them were the descendants of the ancient populations of ancient Aram and Canaan – Hellenised, Romanised, baptised and ultimately converted to Islam. It appears that in the north, in the principalities of Antioch and Edessa, the Moslem population was thinner than in the county of Tripoli and the kingdom of Jerusalem. The proximity of Byzantium, as well as the fact that three hundred years of Moslem domination were followed by a hundred years of Byzantine rule almost to the eve of the crusader conquest, may account for the survival, or even reconversion, of large parts of the Christian population. The situation was radically different in the south, in the Latin kingdom, which had been cut off from Byzantium for more than four centuries by the time the crusaders arrived. Whatever the demographic distribution, however, even in areas in which Islam was not dominant, its language was the common tongue of the population. Arabic was spoken not only by Moslems, but by Christians of every sect and Jews and Samaritans. In the eighth century, the time of the famous Harun al-Rashid, Arabic had ousted Greek and Syriac, which found refuge in the sacred services but relinquished their position in government, street and bazaar. What happened to the language also happened to dress. Laymen of all religions wore the same oriental garb unless constrained by official legislation to dress otherwise.

Moslems were found in the cities as well as in the countryside. But whereas they may have been a minority in the Crusader capitals like Edessa, Antioch and Tripoli, they were quite numerous in the smaller urban centres. Almost immediately after the Crusader conquest, which was accompanied by wholesale massacres and the expulsion of the native population of the cities (very often Moslems, Jews and Christians, as the crusaders did not distinguish between them because of their identical dress), the Moslems resettled in the cities. The only exception was Jerusalem. Here the crusaders decreed that it would be sacrilegious for those who profaned the name of the Messiah to live in the city of His Passion.

The countryside was overwhelmingly Moslem, and the Moslem village (and urban) communities continued to function under Crusader rule. Though the Moslem state had lost its sovereignty and authority, the basic social cells remained. Religious life centred in the villages around the small mosques, and qadis or ulemas probably continued to officiate, as they were indispensable in marriages and succession. Some mosques, even in the larger cities, escaped being converted into churches and remained in the hands of the Moslems. Moreover, the crusaders recognised the traditional authority of the elders, and the raïs (the patriarchal head of the community) was vested with some kind of authority and represented the village in its dealings with the crusader lord. If there was no steward, to supervise the seigniorial revenues, the raïs confirmed by the Franks bore this responsibility as well.

The meeting of the Frankish lord with the Moslems was not only that of rulers and ruled but, on the economic level, that of exploiters and exploited. Strangely enough, this aspect of their relationship was far less harsh than one would tend to assume. The following quotation from a Moslem traveller, Ibn Jubair, who journeyed with a caravan from Damascus to Acre on his way to Tunis, is illuminating. Between Beit Jenn, at the foot of the snow-clad Mount Hermon, and Baniyas, he crossed the frontier into the Latin kingdom. Passing through the Crusader fortress of Tibnin he came upon:

> . . . a road which went through contiguous farms, all inhabited by Moslems who live in great prosperity under the Franks (God preserve us from temptation!). Their obligations are the payment of half the crop at the time of harvest and the payment of a poll-tax of one dinar and five qirats [24 qirats equalled a dinar]. The Christians do not demand anything more, but for a light tax on fruit. But the Moslems are masters of their habitations and and rule themselves as they see fit. This is the situation in farms and villages inhabited by the Moslems in the whole area occupied by the Franks on the shores of Syria. The Moslems are chagrined seeing the state of their co-religionaries in the provinces ruled by the Moslems, as their situation is precisely the opposite of security and happiness. One of the troubles which afflict the Moslems is that under their own government they must always complain about the injustice of their chiefs, whereas they cannot but praise the behaviour of the enemy, on whose justice they can rely.

In the cities, the Moslems undoubtedly found themselves in a more precarious situation as they were a despised and permanently suspected minority among the Franks. Still, Ibn Jubair's sensitivity to the pigs wandering the streets of the Christian cities and the crosses on every corner did not prevent Damascene Moslems and merchants from Mosul from maintaining branches of their businesses in the great Christian emporia on the coast.

There is no doubt that the Moslem aristocracy and intelligentsia, usually city dwellers, disappeared in the wake of the Crusader conquest, leaving the fellaheen, artisans and merchants. Yet the crusaders knew the Moslem upper class quite well. Moslem rulers or the sons of ruling dynasties visited the Frankish cities; the pious visited their holy places; and geographers, doctors and other members of the intelligentsia were not unknown among the Franks. In time a curious kind of relationship developed between the crusader barons and the Moslem rulers. Neither accepted the other in terms of culture or behaviour, but there was a kind of mutual respect between the upper strata of both societies, similar to the respect of the hereditary warrior for his brother-in-arms, albeit an enemy.

Besides the Sunnite and Shi'ite Moslems, a few, curious European travellers knew that in the Lebanon mountains lived a Moslem sect known as the Druze. Founded in the eleventh century, the sect believed that the Fatimid caliph al-Hakim was the last incarnation of the godhead, and they expected his return.

Far more famous was another Moslem sect, the imbibers of the hemp extract hashish, hence called *Hashishiin* or Assassins. A sect of extremists, its members would use any means, murder not excluded, to protect their interests. In time they became a menace to Christian and Moslem alike. William of Tyre, a native of the Holy Land and its greatest historian, described the Assassins as follows:

In the province of Tyre in Phoenicia and in the diocese of Tortosa there lives a tribe of people who possess ten fortresses with the villages attached to them. Their number, as we have often heard, is about sixty thousand, possibly more. It is the custom of this people to choose their ruler not by hereditary right, but by the prerogative of merit. This chief, when elected, they call the Old Man, disdaining a more dignified title. Their subjection and obedience to him is such that they regard nothing [he demands] as too harsh or difficult and eagerly undertake even the most dangerous tasks at his command. For example, if there happens to be a prince who has incurred the hatred or distrust of this people, the chief places a dagger in the hand of one or several of his followers. Those thus designated hasten away at once, regardless of the consequences of the deed or the chances of personal escape. They labour zealously for as long as may be necessary until the favourable chance comes which enables them to carry out the mandate of the chief.

And Marco Polo gives the following description:

Now no man was allowed to enter the garden [of the Old Man] save those whom he intended to be his Ashishin. There was a fortress at the entrance to the garden, strong enough to resist all the world, and there was no other way to get in. He kept at his court a number of the youths of the country, from twelve to twenty years of age, such as had a taste for soldiering . . . Then he would introduce them into his garden, some four, or six or ten at a time, having first made them drink a certain potion which cast them into a deep sleep and then causing them to be lifted and carried in. So when they awoke they found themselves in the garden.

When therefore they awoke and found themselves in a place so charming, they deemed that it was Paradise in very truth. And the ladies and damsels

The great art of the Levant: haggling and conversation. Two Moslem gentlemen in a lively dispute from Ibn Wasiti's illumination of al-Hariri's *Maqamat* (23)

opposite, above The slave market in the Moslem Orient, where black males and white girls were bought for ready money or precious stones (25)

opposite, below Mameluk nobles fighting and hunting together with their household servants, depicted on the 'Baptistère de St Louis', a 14th-century brass vessel inlaid with silver (26)

above A Moslem noblewoman with company on the roads of the Orient (24)

right The pleasures of the Orient: eating, drinking, singing and telling tales of bygone heroic days in festive company (27)

above The Holy History as seen by an
oriental Christian and reproduced on a
brass canteen inlaid with silver (28)

opposite Far from the Caucasus, the
Georgians clung to a foothold in Jerusalem.
The frescoës in the Monastery of the Holy
Cross depict their national poet, Shotha
Rustaveli, kneeling between St Maximus
the Confessor and St John of Damascus
(29)

above Oriental Christendom with
its own liturgy and customs. A
mid-13th century illumination of a
Syriac manuscript shows a bishop
ordaining a priest (30)

opposite, above The Mameluks, as
depicted by Ritter Conrad
Grünemberg in *A Voyage to the
Holy Land*, 1486 (31)

opposite, below The Ethiopians or
Abyssinians, whose Christian
kingdom gave rise to the legend of
the Kingdom of Presbyter John,
from *A Voyage to the Holy Land* (32)

left The centre of the Armenian
community in the Crusader
kingdom was the Cathedral of
St James in Jerusalem. An illumination
from a Gospel (1287) shows an
archbishop ordaining a deacon (33)

ie mameluken das sind verlougnet cristen
der sind aimer zu allokair an king
Soldans hoff. als man fagt ob den Arg
tusenden. Disser lut vint may von ale
landen da. Vnd es mals fagt man mit
dem aimen Gots tutschen verlougnet haben. Zu

right A shepherd as depicted in a 14th-century Armenian manuscript (34)

below A princely gift from Armenia. Detail from doors carved with Armenian and Arabic inscriptions in the basilica of the Church of the Nativity, Bethlehem, donated by King Hayton of Armenia in 1277 (35)

dallied with them to their hearts' content . . .

So when the Old Man would have any prince slain, he would say to such a youth: 'Go thou and slay so and so; and when thou returnest my angels shall bear thee into Paradise. And shouldst thou die, natheless even so will I send my angels to carry thee back into Paradise.'

Few were the countries in the world where such a large number of sects of so many religions were concentrated in one area. This strange phenomenon, which made the Levant a kind of a showcase of Moslem, Christian and Jewish history, was motivated by many factors. In the case of the Christian creeds, the main reason was political. Theologies which were declared to be heterodoxies and whose followers were persecuted by the orthodox, official creed in the Byzantine Empire found an asylum outside its boundaries. Some were adopted by ethnic groups as their native creeds and thus became national churches. This was the case with the Georgians, Armenians, Copts and Ethiopians. Others did not crystallise in national frameworks but represented large segments of the populations, sometimes whole territorial enclaves, within the vast boundaries of tolerant Islam. Such was the position of the Jacobites, Maronites and Nestorians. Though the medley of Christian sects was to be found in Mesopotamia, Syria and Palestine, it was the Holy City, Jerusalem, which could boast the presence of the greatest variety. The attraction of the cradle of religion was reason enough for every sect in Christendom to hold on to a place in the Holy City. Walking the streets of medieval Jerusalem, scanning the sumptuous churches of the Latins, the many churches of the Greeks and the modest chapels of other sects, one felt as if strolling through a compact museum of ecclesiastical history.

The largest and strongest Christian group was the Greeks, the Orthodox Church of Byzantium. Though its strength was concencentrated in the northern principalities, especially in Antioch, it was also present in the Latin kingdom, and before the arrival of the crusaders it represented the richest and best organised church under the domination of Islam. It is therefore rather paradoxical that the crusaders, who vowed at Clermont to liberate the Byzantine Christians from Turkish danger, should turn not only into rivals but even plunderers. A strange combination of circumstances was responsible for this extraordinary development. In the dogmatic sense, the Greeks were not heretics, they were schismatics, temporarily – as the Latins hoped – separated from Rome. As the rites of the Byzantine church and clergy were valid, minor dogmatic differences and divergencies in liturgical practice could easily have been overlooked. It is precisely this theological conformity which turned out to be decisive in the relations between Latins and Greeks. The Latins could not visualise a situation in which they would be ruled by the sees of the Greek clergy; neither was it possible, on theological grounds, to accept a double – Greek and Latin – hierarchy. Consequently, the Greek patriarch of Antioch was re-placed by a Latin one, and the same happened in Jerusalem almost immediately after the conquest. Having deposed the bishops of the Greek Orthodox Church or declared a vacancy of sees, the crusaders proceeded to install their own bishops and demanded that the Greek clergy acknowledge and submit to the new Latin patriarchs and bishops. The result was a permanent tension between Greeks and Latins. The Greek patriarchs, deprived of their sees, retired to Constantinople and continued their succession in the Byzantine capital as the nominal prelates of the countries conquered by the crusaders. The lower clergy remained in Crusader territory but had to pay lip-service to the Latins.

The establishment of the Latin church was often accompanied by the spoliation of the Greek churches, which was legally justified as the regular succession of the Latins into the former possessions of the Greeks. This process was more evident in the great sanctuaries and the cities than in the countryside. Still, the Greek clergy did not disappear. It maintained separate services in the Holy Sepulchre and in the Church of Nativity in Bethlehem. Moreover, at times when political relations were more cordial – as in the middle of the twelfth century, when a Crusader-Byzantine alliance was in the offing – the Latins saw a Greek patriarch re-installed in the see of Antioch and the Byzantine emperor lavishly spending money on the decoration of the basilica in Bethlehem, where inscriptions proclaimed the new oecumenical spirit.

Whatever the position of the Greek clergy in the sanctuaries, the Greek monasteries usually remained firmly in their hands. The monastic traditions of the Holy Land, together with those of Egypt (the oldest in Christendom), were kept alive in the ancient monasteries in the Judean Desert and on the banks of the Jordan River. Picturesque, isolated, indeed, almost inaccessible, monasteries like Qarantal, Mar Saba and Bar-Koziba, not to mention St Catherine in Sinai, remained the refuge of the monk fleeing this world. The ancient liturgy and Greek chant proclaimed both the permanency of the Orthodox Church and the glory of God.

But whereas Greek clergy was numerous, the Greek Orthodox population, strong in the north, was a rather thin layer in the Latin kingdom proper. It was the following of the Syrian Church that made up the bulk of the Christian population of the kingdom. Though not descendants of the ancient Assyrians, as some crusaders were fond to believe, the Syrians were an ancient population, indigenous to the Holy Land, which had preserved its religious identity and its own hierarchy and clergy under the rule of Islam. A vivid description of these oriental Christians, though marred by the prelates' temper, was preserved by a thirteenth-century bishop of Acre:

There are other men who, since the days of old, have dwelt in the land under divers lords, and borne the yoke of slavery successively under the Romans and Greeks, the Latins and barbarians, the Saracens and the Christians. These men are everywhere slaves, always tributaries, kept by their masters for husbandry and other ignoble uses; they are altogether unwarlike, and helpless as women in battle, save some of them who use bows and arrows, but are unarmed and ready for running away. These men are known as Syrians. They are for the most part untrustworthy, double-dealers, cunning foxes even as the Greeks, liars and turncoats, lovers of success, traitors, easily won over by bribes, men who say one thing and mean another, who think nothing of theft and robbery. For a small sum of money they become spies and tell the secrets of the Christians to the Saracens, among whom they are brought up, whose language they speak rather than any other, and whose crooked ways they for the most part imitate. They have mingled among the heathen, and learned their works. They shut up their wives after the Saracen fashion, and wrap up both them and their daughters with cloths, that they may not be seen. They do not shave their beards as do the Saracens, Greeks, and almost all Easterns, but cherish them with great care, and especially glory in them, holding the beard to be a sign of manhood, an honour to the face, and the dignity and glory of man.

The Syrians use the Saracen language in their common speech, and they use the Saracen script in deeds and business and all other writing, except for the Holy Scriptures and other religious books, in which they use the Greek letters. The Syrians exactly follow the rules and customs of the Greeks in divine service and other spiritual matters, and obey them as their superiors. As for the Latin prelates in whose dioceses they dwell, they obey them in word, but not in deed, and only in outward show say that they obey them, out of fear of their masters according to the flesh; for they have Greek bishops of their own, and would not fear excommunication or any other sentence from the Latins in the least, for they say that all Latins are excommunicate, wherefore they cannot give sentence upon anyone.

Whereas Greeks and Syrians were considered schismatics, other Christian churches were outright heretics. This included the four (all Monophysite) national churches of Georgia, Armenia, Egypt (Copts) and Ethiopia. Yet these oriental churches, with their patriarchs and bishops, often profited from the Crusader conquest. The Monophysites were persecuted by the Greeks within the borders of Byzantium, and their relations with the Byzantine church were no better in places dominated by Islam. Virulent polemics, quarrels and accusations were an everyday occurrence. The Crusader conquest put an end to the petty warfare. The crusaders did not inquire, as a Jacobite patriarch tells us with relish, into the beliefs of the sects. To the Franks, all non-Franks were the same. Moreover, these churches, unlike the Greek church did not represent a political factor, and consequently they carried more favour with the conquerors.

The link between the Monophysite churches and the Holy Land was of long standing. Their establishments had grown quite numerous during the last phases of Byzantine domination in the seventh century. The Moslem conquest was probably responsible for some decline, but the fact that Armenia and Georgia represented political factors in Asia Minor played in their favour. Armenians were numerous in the principality of Antioch and probably made up the bulk of the population in the county of Edessa. Smaller Armenian colonies or individual Armenians were also to be found in the Latin kingdom. Their renown as excellent fighters endeared them to the crusaders. In the middle of the twelfth century, the Armenian King Thoros was even toying with the idea of sending thirty thousand Armenians to settle in the Holy Land and thus make it Christian not only in rule but also in population.

The court of Armenia, which in the thirteenth century adopted French manners and to some extent the French language, was a special mixture of East and West. A Jerusalem monk from Mount Zion who visited the court of Lesser Armenia at the end of the thirteenth century (when Armenia was already tributary to the Mongols), left the following impression of his visit to the king and the catholicos, the patriarch of Armenia:

I lived for three weeks in the palace of the king of Armenia and Cilicia, and there were a few Tartars at his Court; but all the rest of his household were Christians, to the number of about two hundred. I used to see them frequent the church, hear masses, kneel and pray devoutly. Moreover, whenever any of them met me and my companion, they did us great honour by taking off their hats and respectfully bowing to us, greeting us and rising up at our approach.

The chief Prelate of the Armenians and Georgians is called the catholicus. I stayed with him for fourteen days, and he had with him many archbishops and bishops, abbots, and other prelates. In his diet, his clothes and his way of life, he was so exemplary that I have never seen anyone, religious or secular, like him; and I declare of a truth that in my opinion all the clothes that he wore were not worth five shillings sterling, and yet he had exceeding strong castles and great revenues and was rich beyond any man's counting. He wore a coarse red sheep-skin pelisse, very shabby and dirty, with wide sleeves, and under it a gray tunic, very old and almost worn out. Above this he wore a black scapular, and a cheap rough black mantle.

The catholicus and all the other prelates are monks, and throughout all the East no one of any nation can be a prelate unless he be a monk. All monks are greatly revered and honoured. Clerks and priests have no authority, neither do the laity pay any regard to them, and they have no duties save celebrating divine service. They mark all the canonical hours by beating a plank or other piece of wood, because they have no bells. When notice is given at night, they go to matins calling out to the people as they go through the streets to come to matins. The Armenian and Georgian priests are distinguished from the laity by a white linen cloth, which they wrap round their neck and shoulders.

Thieves who are guilty of petty thefts, or other evildoers who commit the lesser sorts of crime, are castrated, that they may not beget children to imitate their fathers' misdeeds. This seems to me to be one reason why there are so many courtesans there, for there are many eunuchs there, and all of them are in the service of noble ladies. I believe that the queen of Armenia had more than forty eunuchs when I was at her palace. No man visits her save by the king's special leave, and the king assigns to him some eunuch by name to show him in. So likewise is the custom with all noble ladies, both widows and married.

The great shrine of the Armenians in the Holy Land was the cathedral of St James in the Armenian quarter of Jerusalem. A sanctuary which stood here in the seventh century, and perhaps even earlier, was rebuilt under Crusader rule (around the middle of the twelfth century) and it has served the community uninterruptedly for eight hundred years up to our own times. A wide-spanned triple arcade in the southern part of the sanctuary lead into a narthex, whence a beautiful gate in Crusader romanesque brought the pious to the three-naved sanctuary. With the gilded Chair of St James near the altar and its holy relic, the

head of St James, in a northern chapel, the sanctuary symbolised the
Armenian ties with the church of the Apostles and with the Holy City.
In the fourteenth century the kings of Spain, who took interest in the
sanctuary as the body of St James was venerated in Santiago de Compostela, redecorated the interior of the cathedral.

The Armenians' neighbours in the Caucasus Mountains were the
Georgians. Their ties with the Holy Land were as old as those of their
neighbours. By the end of the fifth century, a Georgian monastery
had been built in the valley which led to Jerusalem. Rebuilt by Justinian
in the sixth century, it remained in the hands of the Georgians during
the Moslem domination, acquiring the name of the Monastery of the
Cross. An old and pious legend had it that the tree from which the
branches of the True Cross were cut grew on the site of the monastery.
The legend probably rests on the story that the queen of David II
the Restorer (d. 1125) founded a nunnery for Georgian ladies in
Jerusalem and sent to the Holy City a piece of the Holy Cross. A part
of it was sent on to Paris by a Frankish monk called Anselm and was
preserved in the cathedral of Notre Dame up to the eve of the French
Revolution. A section of what remained after the revolutionary icono-
clasm was presented to Napoleon and later on to Charles X of France.
The rest is still in the cathedral of Notre Dame. Though lost in the mountains of Judea and only little known outside the country, the Georgian
sanctuary won for itself a special place in the hearts of the brave
Georgians. In the beginning of the thirteenth century, the famous
queen Tamara (d. 1211) sent gifts to the Georgian congregation
in Jerusalem, with a man named Shotha Rustaveli. He remained in
the monastery until his dying day and there composed the greatest
national poem of Georgia, *The Man in the Leopard's Skin* (*Vapkiss
Tokossani*). Generation after generation, this poem has been taught and
recited in the villages and cities of Georgia. Some years ago, a mission
from Georgia (now the Soviet Republic of Grusia) had the good
fortune to uncover in the monastery medieval frescoes depicting its
saints, rulers and the national poet of Georgia.

Another Monophysite church, with a numerous following in almost
all Crusader principalities was the Jacobite Church, so called after its
founder, Jacob Baradaeus. Although this church never crystallised as
the creed of a state or a defined ethnic group, this fact did not prevent
its followers from calling themselves a 'nation'. More numerous in the
north than in the south, their great sanctuary, the monastery of Bar

Sauma, was in Moslem territory. Their patriarch, however, was in Antioch, and as a rule his relations with other Monophysite churches were rather cordial. Moreover, as the most outstanding opponents of the Greeks outside Byzantium, the Jacobites were rather favoured by the crusaders. They maintained their own monasteries and churches in the major cities of the Crusader kingdom, but it was the monastery of Mary Magdalene, built at the end of the eleventh century by the Egyptian Copts, which was their rallying point in the Holy City.

Of the many Christian sects which existed under Crusader rule, none grew closer to the rulers than the Maronites. This sect, like a sediment of history deposited in the mountains and valleys of Lebanon, accepted one of the many doctrines which rent the Church in the seventh century. The doctrine was condemned by the Church as monothelitism (the sectarians asserted one will only, the Divine, in Christ), and its followers found refuge far from Constantinople in the recesses of Lebanon. Like many other doctrines, it was adopted by an ethnic group in Lebanon, and with the Moslem conquest and the separation of Lebanon from Byzantium, it became the national creed of the Christian peasants of ancient Phoenicia. In 1184 the Lebanese Christians abjured monothelitism and accepted the supremacy of the Roman see. This was a momentous event, if not in ecclesiastical history, certainly in that of Lebanon. Despite periods of estrangement, the Christians of Lebanon remained in communion with Rome and were thus far more open to European influences than any other Christian sect in the Levant, a situation which continues to the present.

Pagan Rome, Christian Byzantium, Moslem Arabs and Turks each dominated the Holy Land, and in each age the indigenous population converted to the creed of the ruling power. Yet the efforts at conversion never affected the entire population. Although paganism disappeared entirely, both Christianity and Judaism survived like isolated islands in the sea of Islam.

It is impossible to know how many of the Jewish inhabitants of the Holy Land during the Crusader era were direct descendants of the ancient autochtonous population and how many were newly settled in the country. Generally speaking, it seems that the small Jewish communities in Galilee might trace their origin to the Second Commonwealth, which came to an end with the destruction of the Temple by Titus (AD 71).

Like Islam and Christianity, Judaism had its sects. The Samaritans, who concentrated around Nablus in Samaria, never abandoned their holy Mount Gerizim, and the annual Passover sacrifice was and remains a symbol of their survival and permanence. In the eighth century, the Karaites, a sect founded by Ben Anan, rejected the codes of the Mishna and Talmud and advocated the sole authority of the Holy Scriptures. The heresy spread through the Orient, and very soon the Karaites and Jews, (nicknamed 'Rabbanites'), were writing virulent pamphlets against each other.

The hope and expectation of salvation and return was not confined to the 'Rabbanite' Jews. A Karaite scholar from Jerusalem in the tenth century addressed the following appeal to the Karaite communities:

Brothers! Jerusalem lays in ruins, black, exiled and abandoned, whereas you rest and are asleep on your beds. She is drunk but not from wine and cries out for her sons and the ingathering of the orphans. They wear sacks, fast and suffer, their skin shrunk on their bones. They left their business, forgot their families, left their native countries and live here on dry bread, foregoing meat and wine. They cling to the law of the Lord and they guard His gates, they climb the Mt of Olives and weep.

Let it be known, brothers, that Jerusalem today is the refuge of every man who runs away and a haven to all mourners and a repose to the poor and wretched. God's servants gather in her, one from a city and two from a family and the women are weeping and mourning in the holy language [Hebrew] and in the language of Persia and that of Ismael.

Jews, Karaites and Samaritans all suffered during the Crusader conquest. The news of the approaching First Crusade, which left a bloody trail of Jewish massacres in Europe, preceded the armies. Many a community in the Orient feared the worst. At this hour of reckoning, Jew, Karaite and Moslem joined forces to defend their cities, and in the cases of Jerusalem and Haifa they paid a dear price to bar the invaders. Few urban communities survived the conquest. The Karaites disappeared altogether, probably because they were concentrated in the cities. But the Jews who lived in the villages of Galilee and the Samaritans around Nablus came through the conquest all but intact. Not only was Jewish life not extinguished in the historical home, it actually began to flourish. The crusaders treated the Jews as they did all non-Franks; as second-rate citizens nonetheless permitted

opposite 'The Vardapet (Wise Man) Isaiah teaching', from a 13th-century Armenian manuscript

to pursue their own ways of life and worship. This attitude created a favourable climate, and coupled with the improved facilities of communication with Europe, the Jewish communities were rebuilt. In the thirteenth century there was even a great revival of Jewish life in the Holy Land.

The only official act of discrimination against the Jews was the prohibition against settling in Jerusalem, and even so, Jews employed as dyers did settle there under the crusaders. The turning point came with Saladin's conquest in 1187, when the new ruler of the Moslem East appealed to the Jews to return to the Holy City. The Spanish-Jewish poet Judah al-Harizi, who visited Jerusalem some years later, phrased the proclamation in biblical terms: 'And so he [Saladin] ordered to let it be known in every city, to the great and simple alike: speak ye unto the heart of Jerusalem, that anyone from the seed of Ephraim, whoever wants it, should be free to settle therein.' Very soon Jewish migration to Jerusalem and the Holy Land swelled into a movement, and in the thirteenth century the great luminaries of Judaism, like Yehiel of Paris and Nahmanides from Spain, left their native countries to settle in the Holy Land. The Jewish community of Jerusalem flourished again, though the greatest concentration of Jews was in the maritime cities of Tyre and Acre. By the close of the thirteenth century, when the Latin kingdom was nearing its end, a pupil of Nahmanides was prophesying the imminent arrival of the Messiah!

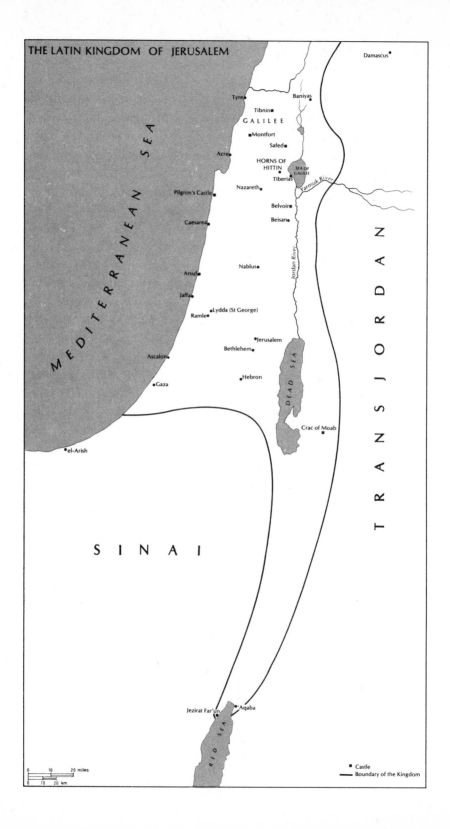

THE LATIN KINGDOM OF JERUSALEM

Damascus

Tyre
Baniyas
Tibnin

GALILEE

Montfort
Safed

Acre

HORNS OF
HITTIN

SEA OF
GALILEE

Pilgrim's Castle
Nazareth
Tiberias

YARMUK RIVER

Belvoir
Beisan

Caesarea

Jordan River

Nablus

Arsuf

Jaffa
Lydda (St George)
Ramle

Jerusalem
Bethlehem

Ascalon

DEAD SEA

Gaza
Hebron

Crac of Moab

el-Arish

T R A N S J O R D A N

S I N A I

Jezirat Far'un
Aqaba

RED SEA

MEDITERRANEAN SEA

0   10   20 miles
0   10   20 km

■ Castle
── Boundary of the Kingdom

5

Ideals and Realities

The Latin kingdom of Jerusalem was established, Frankish colonies had struck roots from Cilicia to the Red Sea and unrelenting Crusader incursions into Moslem territory made it clear that the Westerners had come to the Orient to stay. By the second decade of the twelfth century, European implantation was a *fait accompli*, but its character was undefined and its permanency far from assured. Once the First Crusade was over and its leaders began their journey homewards, taking with them the greater part of the surviving participants, the newly established colonies began to form their political institutions and social organisation, while economic machinery was geared to the needs of the new society.

As early as during the siege of Jerusalem, ideals and expectations had begun to clash with realities. The question of what to do after the imminent conquest was debated amid the din of battering rams and flying stones in the shadow of the besieged city walls. Should the host elect a patriarch before electing a lay ruler, since spiritual values had precedence over the lay ones? Or should no one be elected, since the conquest of the city would surely usher in the Kingdom of Christ and precipitate the descent of Heavenly Jerusalem on this vale of tears? The decision was postponed, but once the city was taken and the victorious host had celebrated mass in the Church of the Resurrection, the problem had to be dealt with. The decision was to elect a lay ruler, Godfrey of Bouillon, as 'Defender of the City' and 'Advocate of the Holy Sepulchre'. He was not a king, and his rule and title were not permanent. This was the compromise between clashing claims and aspirations. The election itself was a milestone in the ideology of the Crusading movement; but when confronted with realities, the ideals had not emerged unscathed. Despite the messianic glimmer which accompanied the birth of the kingdom, its future as a lay state, no different from any other, was sealed. Recognition of this fact, in turn, dampened the messianic *élan* of the Crusader movement. Jerusalem was destined to exist as earthly Jerusalem, and Zion meant no more than a hill in the mountains of Judea.

Within the framework of the European establishments in the Orient, four political entities came into being. The northernmost Crusader state was the county of Edessa, situated between the upper Tigris and the Euphrates rivers. It was the most curious of the Crusader establishments. Edessa was inhabited mainly by oriental Christians who had preserved their identity, despite isolation from the Byzantine Empire and successive waves of Turkoman and Turkish conquerors. In addition to the Armenians and Jacobites, who made up the bulk of the population, there were 'Syrians', Nestorians and other smaller Christian communities. This conglomeration of Christian sects and churches was ruled by Baldwin, brother of Godfrey of Bouillon, who implanted a Lotharingian dynasty in what is now the territory of Iraq. An oriental Christian principality ruled by Western Latins with enclaves of Moslem population in the cities and countryside, Edessa faced the two great Moslem centres, Mosul and Baghdad, as the Crusader bulwark in the north-east.

To the west was the principality of Antioch. Its western frontier was the Syrian seaboard with the ports of St Simeon (Antioch) and Laodicea. Its northern frontiers bordered on the generally friendly Armenian principalities of the Taurus Mountains. It was in the east that Antioch faced the great emporia of Islam: Aleppo and the cities of Homs and Hama. At the zenith of its expansion, the principality reached the very gates of the Moslem capitals, and from time to time the rulers of Aleppo were obliged to pay tribute to the Antiochenes even for the use of the mills just outside the gates of their capital. The Antiochenes tried to maintain bridgeheads and strongholds across the Orontes River, but relied mainly on the defences on the river's bank. The principality could not dominate vast territories, and in practice the Orontes served as the frontier between Antioch and its Moslem neighbours.

It is impossible to know whether the bulk of the principality's population was Moslem or Christian, but it has been surmised that oriental Christians made up the majority. The Christians of Antioch belonged to three main denominations: the Byzantine Church; the 'Syrian' Church, which in dogma and liturgy was Greek but whose adherents spoke Arabic; and finally the Monophysite Church of the Jacobites, which used a Syriac liturgy and Arabic in everyday life. The Moslem population, partly Arab and partly Turkish but mostly descendants of Hellenized Syrians who had adopted Islam, could be found in the cities as well. Mainly, however, the Moslems inhabited the countryside. To this ethnic and religious pastiche, the crusaders added themselves. When Bohemond became its first ruler, Antioch was recognised as the domain of the Normans of southern Italy and Sicily. Naturally, in later waves of European migration, the south Italian Normans, and probably the Normans of France and England as well, were drawn to the principality ruled by their native dynasty. The Normans were not the only European element in Antioch, but they were certainly the dominant one.

The smallest of the Crusader establishments was the Lebanese county of Tripoli, so named after its capital city. Wedged between the sea in the west and the mountain ranges of Lebanon in the east, it enjoyed peaceful borders with two Crusader states, Antioch in the north and Jerusalem in the south. The greater part of its population was Moslem, and the entire native population spoke Arabic. Sects of the oriental churches, especially the Jacobites, made up a significant part of the population, but the distinctive religious group in the county was the Maronites. Famous as excellent archers, these Christian farmers preserved their ancestral faith and their community organisation. The county of Tripoli was governed by Provençals. It was Raymond of St Gilles, count of Toulouse and marquis of Provence, who implanted his dynasty in Lebanon. In parlance and custom, Lebanon thus became southern French, a haven for those from the lower Rhone to the Pyrenees – and even as far as Catalonia – who settled in the new, Christian Near East.

The fourth political entity was the kingdom of Jerusalem proper. The prestigious name of the capital conferred upon its ruler the rank and title of king and a kind of precedence, even hegemony, over other Crusader establishments. The house of Bouillon (i.e., of lower Lorraine) ruled the kingdom until Fulk v, count of Anjou, married the heiress of the kingdom, Queen Melissande, and established the Angevine dynasty. Later, the ruling house became Poitevin through marriage. The first ruler of the kingdom, Godfrey of Bouillon, was titled 'Defender of the Holy Sepulchre', but his brother and successor, Baldwin i, was crowned king of Jerusalem in the Church of the Nativity in Bethle-

hem, thus underscoring his claim to the royal inheritence of King
David. With more daring than modesty, Baldwin I even entitled
himself 'king of Asia and Egypt', a bit of wishful thinking which
almost came true under one of his successors (King Amalric). Although
the Crusader kings of Jerusalem never became rulers of Asia and Africa,
the extent of their kingdom was ultimately the largest among the
Western establishments.

From the northern border with the county of Tripoli at the small
al-Mu'amaltain River close to Byblos, the kingdom extended along
the Phoenician and Palestinian coast down to the desert which divides
the Holy Land from Sinai. Its coastal cities were the glory of ancient
and classical history: Beirut, Sidon, Tyre, Acre, Apollonia (Arsuf),
Caesarea, Jaffa, Ascalon and Gaza. Some of the cities, like Beirut,
Tyre, Acre and Jaffa, developed and flourished under the crusaders
as major emporia of international commerce. Inland, the frontier of
the kingdom cut eastwards through the Lebanese mountains to the
headwaters of the Jordan. An undefined frontier on the Golan Heights
marked the north-eastern border. From here it extended some 300
miles south to the Red Sea at 'Aqaba, encompassing Transjordan
(the ancient Gilead, Ammon and Moab) on its eastern flank.

Shaped like a square shield with a pointed base, the kingdom was
a wedge inserted between the two centres of Moslem power: the great
Syrian capital of Damascus, ruled by Seljuq Turks and adhering to the
Sunnite caliphate of Baghdad; and Cairo, the Fatamid capital of the
powerful Shi'ite caliphate of Egypt. In the south, the crusaders reached
the Sinai desert oasis of el-Arish and their armies even penetrated the
delta of the Nile several times. But the kingdom's borders were finally
stabilised in the east and south along the fringes of the deserts of Syria
and Transjordan and the Negev and Sinai, which served as natural
frontiers.

The population of the kingdom of Jerusalem was probably more
heterogeneous than that of the Crusader principalities of the north.
The Holy Places, as well as the influence of religious institutions,
preserved enclaves of Christians, Jews and Samaritans among the
Moslem population. In places like Jerusalem, Bethlehem, Nazareth
and possibly Mount Tabor, the Christian population was large,
perhaps even dominant. The same was true of some rural districts
around Jerusalem and in Galilee. There was scattered Jewish settlement
in rural Galilee and organised Jewish communities in every major

city of Palestine and Syria. Still, after four hundred years of Moslem rule, the country was Islamised; and even where the dominant religion did not have the upper hand, its language did: Arabic was the common language of all inhabitants, regardless of religion. An early attempt to write Greek in Arabic letters failed, but for hundreds of years Arabic was written by oriental Jews in Hebrew letters.

In Jerusalem, the southernmost Crusader establishment, the ethnic composition of the Western population was far more varied than in the north. The attraction of the Holy Places counter-balanced the natural tendency to settle among kinfolk. The ruling dynasty and the original nucleus of European population came from north-eastern and central France, but later waves of immigration brought in Provençals and Angevins. The streets of twelfth-century Jerusalem or thirteenth-century Acre were a kaleidoscopic microcosm of contemporary Europe and the Near East. The predominant French brushed shoulders with members of other ethnic and linguistic groups who lived in special quarters or streets, often no more than a few houses clustered around a church dedicated to a particularly popular patron saint in the homeland. The Spaniard and Provençal, Italian, German, Hungarian and Breton each eked out a place for himself.

Whereas in a city like Jerusalem, with its many ecclesiastical institutions, the overwhelming majority of the inhabitants were Westerners, a large native population, attracted by economic prospects, resettled in the maritime cities after the Crusader conquest. Moslems who fled or were expelled during the conquest returned and settled in almost every city of the kingdom, with the exception of Jerusalem. And where Moslems were less prominent, there were Arabic-speaking oriental Christians, who wore the same dress and headgear. The Monophysite Armenians had their own quarters; Georgians, Jacobites, Copts and Ethiopians maintained their own churches; and Byzantines and Syrians met with Maronites and Nestorians. Druze and Bedouin were also found in the bazaars or market-places of the cities exchanging their pastoral products or selling their services. Except for Christian enclaves, the countryside was predominantly Moslem, especially in the regions of Judea, Samaria and Galilee, which in any case were less attractive to the Westerners than the coastal cities and their fortifications.

The messianic ideals and expectations had vanished. Heavenly intervention was still hoped for, but each and every day the small, conquering minority was faced with a struggle for survival. Constant vigilance had to be maintained against attack from without or revolt and sabotage from within. At first there was little choice: state and society had to be organised for war. Royal and princely powers were reduced to those of military commanders. For almost a generation, it was the commanders who went to war, defended the frontiers, built the fortifications and made peace. Only after this settling-in period did a machinery of government emerge from the war-oriented Crusader camp.

All in all, the kingdom of Jerusalem could put into the field some six hundred knights and ten times as many foot soldiers. Antioch and Tripoli together could have put a similar number into the field. Today, 1,200 knights might seem an insignificant force, but in the Middle Ages the heavily mailed, mounted knight had approximately the same combat effectiveness as a modern tank. Tancred, for example, almost reached Damascus with eighty knights, and King Amalric invaded Egypt with only about three hundred. In Europe as well, major contemporary battles were being fought with similar or even smaller contingents. In addition, the kingdom had at its disposal the forces of the military orders, which could raise an army as strong as that of the kingdom itself. And, of course, during the great crusades, thousands of European knights reached the shores of the Christian Levant, swelling the available military manpower.

In a pitched battle, the Crusader armies were almost invincible, and in actual fact they were seldom defeated. But a single defeat had a different meaning to the crusaders than to their antagonists. The latter had almost inexhaustible manpower reserves. To them, the most crushing defeat meant no more than a lost campaign, followed by a retreat to distant, secure bases beyond the reach of the Crusader armies in Aleppo, Damascus or Cairo. For the crusaders, who in cases of a major attack had to mobilise almost all their manpower, a defeat could mean the loss of a battle, a war or even the kingdom itself. This is exactly what happened in July 1187 at the battle of Hittin, when defeat did mean the loss of the kingdom.

The success of conquest, implantation and defence depended directly on the all-important question of manpower. This problem, more than any other, demonstrated the greatest failure of the Crusades and proved to be the paramount reason for the ultimate bankruptcy of the Latin establishments in the East. When the leaders of the First Crusade left the Holy Land for home, the remaining settlers and their leaders,

✠ ANNON : DOV : SAINT : ESP
T : IE : BEIMONT : PAR : LA : CR
SE : DE : DEV : PRINCE : DANT
OOLIS : CONTE : DE : TRIPLE
IS : FAIRE : SYSC . . . TOR : DE
LA MONEE : DE LA : QUMVIIA
TE : DES : GENS : DE TRIP
N : LITN : DE : LINCARNAS
TRE : SENIOR : I
. . . M : CC : LXVI

'In the name of the Holy Spirit, I, Bohemond, by the grace of God, prince of
Antioch and count of Tripoli, ordered the erection of this Tower of the Mint
of the Commune of Tripoli. In the year of the Incarnation of our Lord,
MCCLXVI . . .' (36)

above A constitutional crisis. Young King Baldwin III refuses the tutelage of Queen Melissande (37)

left A man kneeling in prayer, from a tombstone erected in Acre in 1290, a year before the fall of the city (38)

right The unavoidable clash between crown and mitre is depicted by the prince of Antioch imprisoning the patriarch of the city (39)

overleaf The mighty citadel of Aleppo, the Moslem bulwark against Antioch (40)

above Christendom was in a permanent state of war along the frontiers of Islam. A Christian city on alert bristles with knights in full armour in this illumination from an early 13th-century Spanish manuscript (41)

right Le roi est mort, vive le roi! The clergy attend the death of the king of Jerusalem and the patriarch of Jerusalem anoints his successor. From a 13th-century Crusader manuscript written in Acre (42)

above The art of the Latin West was transplanted under oriental skies. The raising of Tabitha by St Peter (Acts, 9, 36–43) represented on a romanesque capital in Nazareth (43)

left Gaza of biblical fame became the southern outpost of the Crusader kingdom. The romanesque portal of the Crusader cathedral (12th century), which has now become a mosque (44)

Seal of the king of Jerusalem showing the city's three major landmarks:
the Dome of the Rock, the citadel and the Holy Sepulchre (45)

Godfrey of Bouillon, Bohemond, Raymond of St Gilles, Baldwin and Tancred, expected a new crusade and mass migration from Europe to furnish the manpower necessary to complete the conquest of the Near East. The attraction of the Holy Places, the majestic image of a Christian state in the cradle of its religion and the inducement and temptation of the mysterious and opulent East left the remaining settlers assured that they would not be abandoned. But their expectations were disappointed. A new crusade, set rolling in 1101, ground to a halt in the sands of Asia Minor. Though the hosts of the Second and Third Crusades tried to cross Asia Minor again, their attempts ended in greatest hardship and calamity. In the twelfth century, long-distance communication was effected by sea. Large-scale transport, on the other hand, was carried overland. The restriction of the crusades to sea routes was dangerous and, above all, limited the possibilities for mass migration. Twelfth-century maritime facilities, at their best, could never replace land transport.

There was more than technical difficulties crippling development of the kingdom's manpower resources. After the great awakening of the First Crusade, Europe's responses to the kingdom's appeals never met its needs. Instead of the expected floods of settlers, only a thin trickle made its way to the East. Only those crusades which took place in the wake of calamities, like the loss of Edessa (1146) or the fall of Jerusalem (1187), brought thousands to the Levant again. But of the masses which participated in the great crusades, only a very thin sediment remained in the country. Once their vows were fulfilled, newcomers would abandon the kingdom for their European homelands. Six months after the capture of Jerusalem in 1099, the crusaders could scarcely settle a quarter of their capital. This was a grim reality. The tangible results of continuing immigration were probably more apparent during periods of relative peace between the great crusades than during them. It was calculated that after four generations, at the time of the battle of Hittin (1187), some 120,000 crusaders lived in the kingdom of Jerusalem and about the same number inhabited the northern principalities. In all, a quarter of a million Europeans were established in the Levant. Because the short medieval life-span was even shorter in the Latin East – due to the climate, food, maladjustment and the permanent state of siege and war – the waves of immigration were simply not sufficient to make the Christian colonies viable political entities.

The crusaders were outnumbered approximately five to one inside their own boundaries. While this statistical evaluation proves that the Crusades failed at colonisation, it is far more significant when viewed in the geo-political framework of the Near East, where the quarter of a million Europeans faced not only the Moslem inhabitants of their dominions, but also the millions from the Nile to Mesopotamia. Fortunately for the crusaders, Islam was unable to mobilise its resources for more than a hundred and fifty years. The bonds of common religion, language and culture could not undo history and experience. Attempts, like those of Saladin, to unite the forces of Islam, were short-lived and rarely survived their originator. Only the military dictatorship of the Mameluk general Baybars, in the middle of the thirteenth century, could create a unified state, and then only by ruthlessly enforcing strict uniformity.

Outnumbered, the crusaders were doomed to remain a ruling minority in an almost permanent state of war. Logic and caution dictated that they concentrate in a few positions, all of them fortified. This became a major characteristic of the Crusader kingdom. Whereas in their homelands lord and serf almost always lived in the countryside, in the Orient the Latins took to fortified cities and castles almost without exception. Here and there a fortified manor-house, never too far from a castle or fortified city, testified to rural Crusader settlement. But Crusader villages populated by Western immigrants were a rarity, and in any case they were never without a defence tower, unless they huddled in the shadow of a fortress.

It was from these fortified centres, usually cities, that the crusaders ruled the country. To make their presence felt and their domination effective, the crusaders dotted all major roads and passes with small forts that resembled observation points or police outposts. This network of fortifications, one of the most elaborate the country had ever seen, became the stone-and-iron grid of the kingdom. As long as the castles, forts and strongholds remained intact, the crusaders ruled the Holy Land. But they ruled it only insofar as their citadel-garrisons, castle guards and road patrols could police the country. A clear indication of the shortcomings of Crusader domination made itself evident eighty years after the foundation of the kingdom. A band of Moslems (whose main base was in Damascus) entrenched themselves in the mountains of Upper Galilee and, undisturbed by the Crusader authorities, levied taxes on the local population. It was almost an accident that a royal army, busy fortifying one of the nearby Jordanian passes and provoked by the ambushes of these guerillas, put an end to their activities and destroyed their hide-outs. This sort of incident made it imperative to maintain state and society in a permanent war-like stance. The Heavenly Jerusalem tarried in its descent, and eternal peace remained in the lofty realm of prophecies and dreams. Earthly Jerusalem, despite all the spiritual values for which it stood, had to be ruled and defended by realistic means.

The political régime which evolved in the early Latin kingdom was based upon the feudal system – the only one known to the Westerners – though adapted to meet local circumstances and the particulat challenges and needs of ruling a conquered country. Fiefs – that is land, manors and villages normally accorded by crown and prince to their vassals to assure them an income, the ability to perform their military duties and lead a type of life congruous with their standing in society – were scarce in the beginning. The maintenance of the noble vassals was secured not by land grants, but by income available in the developed monetary economy of the Near East. In addition, the understandable hesitation of the kings to create competitive territorial powers tended to limit the distribution of fiefs. Royal and princely domains were the first to be constituted, and they included all new conquests. But eventually fiefs were created and lordships with local seigniorial dynasties were established. They were unusual in that the city, rather than the castle, served as their centre. Here feudalism adapted itself to the ancient urban traditions of the East. The city became the financial, jurisdictional and administrative centre of the Crusader state, and the lord of the city had to assure that a given number of heavily mailed knights and foot soldiers ('*serjeants*') would be available for the royal host. Guarding castles and maintaining fortifications in the seigniory were also part of the lord's military duties.

Once the vestiges of the early Crusader ideology, its messianic expectations and dependence on ecclesiastical hierarchy were done away with, the process of organising the conquered lands followed in the path of European feudalism. It is rather remarkable that although the developed money economy made it possible to create a bureaucratic monarchy with salaried officials and a paid army, the crusaders nonetheless organised their state according to traditions they had brought from Europe. After a generation of difficulties and uncertainties, the introduction of feudalism as a system of government resulted in a division of the country into a number of princely and seigniorial fiefs dependent on the crown of Jerusalem. Yet the new feudal map did not lead directly to any noticeable weakening of the central power. Too much depended on the ruler and his standing as commander-in-chief of the armies to give free rein to the centrifugal tendencies inherent in the system.

The early Crusader lords and barons were far more disciplined than their European counterparts. This was not the result only of the tense state of permanent emergency but also the peculiar social composition of Crusader nobility. With fewer than half a dozen exceptions, the members of the upper class of nobility who participated in the First Crusade returned to Europe. For some this decision had been taken when they left for the Holy Land; others decided to return only after Jerusalem had been captured. The former took an oath to participate in the crusade and liberate the Holy Sepulchre, and their religious obligations went no farther; once at their journey's end, they felt free to return home. Others, who may have been searching for a chance to carve out a dominion for themselves in the East, were disappointed and preferred their homelands. Those who remained in the Holy Land did not belong to the great houses of European nobility. By and large, they were lower knights of the European lordly households. This in itself facilitated the task of ruling, and the crown of Jerusalem did not face any baronial oppositian during the first generation of the kingdom's existence.

After about three decades, the broad outlines of the feudal map of the kingdom became fixed. At this time the royal domain was still larger, and certainly richer, than the largest fief, probably even richer than all the feudal lordships put together. Almost the whole of Judea between Hebron in the south and ancient Samaria around Nablus in the north was part of the royal domain. At the same time, the crown was overlord of the three main maritime cities of the kingdom, Jaffa, Acre and Tyre, besides the capital, Jerusalem. Facing the large royal domain were the possessions of the tenants-in-chief. Some, like the principality of Galilee, the lordship of Transjordan and the county of Jaffa (later the county of Jaffa-Ascalon, which became an apanage of the royal family) were very large. Others, around the maritime cities of Beirut, Sidon, Haifa, Caesarea and Arsuf or inland centres like Nablus, Hebron, Ramle and Beisan, were small by European standards. Strangely enough, despite the religious motivations behind the Crusades, there were only a few ecclesiastical seigniories – Lydda (called St George), Bethlehem and Nazareth – and these were very small. The usual centre of a seigniory was the city. Exceptions, like the buffer state of Transjordan, had a central castle. The military and administrative centre of the lordship was the lord's lodgings in or near the city citadel. Lodged in the citadel was the city garrison. Often built near the main gate of the city, the citadel also housed the customs officials who taxed incoming products and food stuffs.

The lordships were organised like miniature replicas of the kingdom. The central organ of royal government was the king's court or the High Court, as it was called by the crusaders. Here the king met with his tenants-in-chief, that is his vassals from among the higher nobility. (Technically, knights of the royal household and the vassals in the royal domain were also tenants-in-chief, since they too were direct vassals of the crown.) The royal court, like any other in Christendom, was first and foremost a court of law, dispensing justice to the crown's vassals and dealing with problems related to their noble fiefs and tenures (i.e., the lordships delegated by the crown). More important, the court was the highest council of government. Though originally only an advisory council, it gradually became the decisive political factor in the kingdom. Although the body convened at the king's initiative and the king could choose the matter for discussion, foreign policy, declarations of war and peace, orders for mobilisation and extraordinary (i.e., non-feudal) taxation were all subject to High Court deliberation.

As long as the power of the crown was strong, its voice was decisive. But beginning in the second half of the twelfth century, and even more so during the thirteenth century, the High Court replaced the waning power of the crown. The High Court played an important role during contested royal succession in the twelfth century, and during the thirteenth century, when the legitimacy of the succession was nebulous and contested again, the High Court appropriated more and more competences and became the most important power factor in the kingdom. Its competences and its composition (the court included everybody who was anybody in the kingdom) entirely overshadowed the executive branch of government. The central administration, organised immediately after the conquest, reflected the European tradition which ultimately derived from the time of Charlemagne, when the officers of the royal household – seneschal, constable, chamberlain, butler and the prelate who served as chancellor of the royal chancery – were also officers of state. This primitive framework continued for two centuries with no marked changes. But that testifies as much to the unimportance of the offices as it does to the conservative spirit of the kingdom. Needless to say, royal appointments to these offices were rarely contested. As a matter of fact, the crown appointed members of the highest nobility, almost exclusively, as if serving in such capacities was part of their education in political or public life.

In contrast, the growing importance of the High Court was accompanied by changes in its composition. By the middle of the twelfth century, all fief holders in the kingdom were admitted to the High Court, which meant that, theoretically, it included all the kingdom's nobles, vassals and sub-vassals alike. By the thirteenth century, representatives of some corporate bodies made their appearance, namely the grand masters of the military orders, the consuls or viscounts of the various communes and representatives of a new type of corporate body, the *confrérie* or brotherhood. (The latter, basically charitable associations, with their own patron saint, sometimes open to noble and burgess alike, in several instances became the nucleus of revolutionary movements.) In the last decades of the kingdom, the High Court was on its way to becoming a medieval parliament of the kingdom, uniting participants of different estates with the representatives of corporations.

The lord's court, which brought together the vassals of the lordship and – like the kingdom's High Court – was principally a court of law, was also an advisory council to the lord. The executive organs of the lordship were also copied from those of the crown, but only the great lordships could boast the state's range of officers. Normally, each lordship had its own chancery and an officer or two to deal with the lord's finances and household. But the demographic composition of Crusader lordships differed radically from the European model with which the Crusader noble was familiar. Instead of dealing with European nobles and serfs, the Crusader noble had to deal with knights, burgesses, nationals of the Italian communes and so forth, all lumped into the generic category of Franks, not to mention the oriental Christians of a half a dozen denominations, Moslems, Jews and in some parts of the country Druze, Assassins and Samaritans.

It was an exciting and strange world, and nothing in their earlier experience prepared the crusaders to deal with it. The crusaders, having the adaptability of mere mortals, took the line of least resistance. They simply never mixed socially with the natives and left them to their own governmental devices as well. This was a crucial decision which demanded the renunciation of any state-wide missionary work among the Moslems or oriental Christians. Thus, although the Holy Land was under Christian domination, it never became a Christian country; the majority of its inhabitants remained non-Christian. Once again, reality had clashed with an ideal, and it was reality which had dictated harsh terms of surrender. There was a chance of putting back the clock three hundred years and re-creating the Christian state as it had existed under the Byzantines, before it had been overrun by the swift Bedouin cavalry which surged from the depths of the Arabian peninsula to establish Moslem domination. But the crusaders never used this opportunity: conversion never became a part of the Crusader program, and the waves of European migration never allowed whole-sale replacement of the native population by European colonists.

On the other hand, the principle of non-intervention, which to a large degree perpetuated the tradition of the previous Moslem régime, guaranteed the autonomy of the diverse religious communities. In the villages the members of the different communities were judged before their own traditional, lay or ecclesiastical authorities. This was largely the case in the cities of the kingdom as well. Only in cases that involved Franks and non-Franks, or when a member of a minority wanted recourse to the alien courts, was Frankish jurisdiction available.

One rung down the hierarchy from knights and nobles were the Crusader freemen, or burgesses. From their rank and file a kind of city patriciate came slowly into being, but it was quite different from that of the European cities. The Frankish burgesses never became prominent in the urban economy, as did their European counterparts. The most lucrative occupation, that of international merchant, became a *de facto* monopoly of the Italians, Provençals and Catalans. The Crusader-urban patriciate rose to power not through economic success but rather through the administrative channels. In each city, most conspicuously in Acre and Jerusalem, a number of families rose to power in the en-tourage of patriarch and king, bishop and grand seigneur. They were a class of men who probably received their training in the schools attached to church and monastery under a *magister*, who taught the rudiments of reading, writing and arithmetic. They also acquired a smattering of Latin, just enough to deal with accounts and reports

and jot down the minutes of a contract which would later be elaborated
by the official notaries. Whenever they attempted to write Latin, they
introduced French and Italian expressions and butchered the grammar.
Still, they were efficient and, like their betters from the nobility, they
found a productive outlet for their administrative talents in the courts
of the kingdom set aside for the non-nobles.

The Court of Burgesses and its jurors became the focal point of the
patriciate, and the institution itself became a power in the city. Jurors
enjoyed prestige as the upper crust of the non-noble Franks, and with
the evolution of the court's competences they quickly rose in standing.
The Court of Burgesses, an office of record, became a branch of the
judiciary as the exclusive court for burgesses and their urban properties.
All manner of burgher real-estate transaction, like sales, rents, mort-
gages on houses, city plots, gardens, wells and so on, were recorded;
and cases involving litigations were brought before the jurors of the
court. From sunrise to sunset, three days a week, the jurors sat surrounded by notaries, scribes and beadles, while the entire citizenry
of a Crusader city paraded before them with its problems, from real-
estate litigation through tax evasions, customs evasions, theft and
felony. The city's police superintendent, or *mathesep*, who was responsible for honourable business practices in the bazaars, brought his
culprits here to press charges, and the prison attendants took the
condemned from here to the pillory or prison. In some cases a new
date would be fixed for the parties or a date would be fixed to fight
out the truth in a duel – with sticks, as in burgess tradition.

In time, the city lord found it increasingly profitable and proper
to share his larger competences with the Court of Burgesses. Ordinances
on curfews, prices and cleaning the streets were decided by the court.
Then the town-crier would mount a special stone, usually a part of an
ancient column, called *le ban*, and proclaim them to the assembled
population. Constant attendance at court, while apparently not directly
remunerative, did create among the burgesses a large group of lawyers
or jurists, just as it had among the Crusader nobility. Undoubtedly
knowledgeable, their prestige was so high that even the haughties
among the nobles sought their advice and sometimes invited them to
the feudal court of the kingdom.

opposite The Crusader nobility as depicted in a
statue of Ekkhard and Utah in the Cathedral of
Naumberg, 13th century

Besides the feudal court of the lord and the parallel Court of Burgesses, there was a separate Court of the Market, a mixed Franco-Syrian institution with jurisdiction over petty quarrels in the marketplace in which plaintiff and accused were members of different communities. Long before the establishment of the Court of the Market, there was a native Syrian court, presided over by the *raïs*. According to a Crusader tradition, these courts were perpetuated by the earliest kings of Jerusalem at the request of the native Christian community. As time passed, some of their competences were taken over by the Court of the Market. Such an evolution, partly a function of urban life, did not take place in the villages with oriental Christian or Moslem populations, where the native courts continued to function.

A rather remarkable institution which evolved to meet the new conditions of life was the Court of the Chain. The name derived from the chain used in Crusader maritime cities, as described by the famous Spanish-Jewish traveller Benjamin of Tudela in the last quarter of the twelfth century:

Tyre is a very fine city with a harbour in its midst, and the ships enter the city between two towers. At night, those who levy dues throw iron chains from tower to tower, so that no man can go forth by boat or in any other way to rob the ships by night.

In times of war as well, chains were extended between the jetty towers to prevent enemy ships from entering the harbour. The Court of the Chain was a juridical institution which specialized in maritime cases. Cases involving transport, sailors, shipwrecks, maritime loans and commercial companies certainly required the specialised knowledge of ship captains, who were usually shipowners or merchants as well. Only after the court had clarified the case were the findings transmitted to the Court of Burgesses for judgement and execution.

The development of all these institutions was a far cry from the hopes and aspirations of the First Crusade but was necessary to preserve and rule the kingdom. The king regarded himself as a successor of King David, but he was no more than the ruler of one of the states of Christendom.

The existence of the small Crusader colonies in the East depended entirely on Europe not only for large-scale immigration, but for financial aid as well. Indeed, immigrants from Europe did arrive in the Holy Land, but how different was this immigration from the great

masses of the First Crusade! Their primary motivation was hardly
religious, let alone messianic. Some Europeans went to the East to cast
off the chains of serfdom; others wanted to start a new life in an unknown land with well-publicized possibilities. The messianic tension
of the First Crusade was forgotten, and along with it belief in the
fulfilment of the prophecies of old and the imminence of the Last
Judgement. Europe had lived out its greatest hour of spiritual uplift
and expectation and now resigned itself to the routine, mundane tasks
of living.

But despite the fact that immigration to the East had become socially
and economically motivated, Europe still felt that the distant Crusader
kingdom was more than just another political entity in Christendom.
In a sense it safeguarded not only the Holy Sepulchre but the spiritual
image Europe wanted to project of itself. The Crusader kingdom was
the creation of Europe's finest hour, of the joy of rising above petty
rivalries and fratricidal wars; it was the embodiment of Europe's
belief in and consciousness of the universality of its faith. As long as
these beliefs remained strong, Europe regarded itself as the warden
of its young progeny. For almost two hundred years, albeit with
diminishing fervour, Europe took care of the kingdom, sent immigrants, subsidised the almost permanently empty coffers of Crusader
treasuries and prepared and launched new expeditions to the East.
The two universal powers, empire and papacy, the two heads of
Christendom, temporal and spiritual, took the lead. The kingdom's
claim on Christian Europe was so strong that for generations the papacy
taxed European clergy and laymen in order to assure the necessary
financial means for crusade and kingdom. And kings and princes all
over Europe followed the lead. France and Norman England felt the
strongest bond with the kingdom, but support from Norway, Sicily,
Spain and Hungary. As long as Europe regarded the kingdom as its
own flesh and blood, support continued.

By the beginning of the thirteenth century, however, all this had
changed. New winds began to blow, and the ideal of Universal
Christendom bowed to the rising feudal monarchies. The new vision
of peaceful missions rivalled that of conquest by force. Step by step,
Europe began to sever its emotional links with its oriental colonies,
and only visionaries like St Louis briefly rekindled the old Crusader
enthusiasm. But by then the movement was already doomed.

6

Life in Outremer

The noble and knight brought with them from Europe notions and ideals of the seigniorial life-style and transplanted them in the soil of the newly conquered state. Western Europe perpetuated itself under oriental skies. The French language, fashions and customs struck roots in the Levant, and soon a second and a third generation of the original conquerors and settlers had grown up in the country for whom 'home' meant the Holy Land, whereas Europe – the 'old home' – was a place of their ancestors' far-removed origin. This was a new breed of men and women nicknamed *Poulains*, which should probably be translated or understood in the sense of 'kids'. Their home life, family relations and tutors were all reflections of Europe and, more specifically, France. Yet their environment – the physical conditions of life, the daily meetings in street and bazaar – was the Levant. Thus a scion of a noble, or even a knightly, family underwent the same process of upbringing and education as his European counterpart. He was raised under the mantle of the same religion, instructed in the same tenets of faith, drew his intellectual attitudes and images from the same legends, pious tales, heroic romances and courtly poetry. A *France d'Outremer*, a 'France overseas', was created.

Yet the Syrian-born Frank was not wholly European. Mixed marriages with Armenian and Byzantine ladies were a common occurrence in the upper strata of the Frankish nobility. It was thus considered quite 'normal' that one's mother, grandmother or aunt was an oriental Christian. This was true not only for the nobility but even for the royal and princely Crusader houses. Such a marriage brought with it the oriental servants and attendants – whether Christian or Moslem – which abounded in every wealthy Frankish household. Members of the lower strata of Frankish society, whether simple knights or burgesses, often intermarried with oriental Christians on their own social level. A

Crusader chronicler reflected upon the resultant state of affairs:

... Consider, I pray, and reflect how in our time God has transferred
the West into the East. For we who were Occidentals now have been made
Orientals. He who was a Roman or a Frank is now a Galilean or Palestinian.
One who was a citizen of Rheims or of Chartres now has been made a citizen
of Tyre or Antioch. We have already forgotten the places of our birth;
they have become unknown to many of us or, at least, are unmentioned.
Some already possess homes and servants here which they have received
through inheritance. Some have taken wives not merely of their own people
but Syrians, or Armenians or even Saracens who have received the grace of
baptism. Some have with them a father-in-law, or daughter-in-law, or
son-in-law, or stepson or stepfather. Here, too, are grandchildren and
great-grandchildren. One cultivates vines, another fields. Both use the
speech and the idioms of different languages. These languages, now made
common, become known to both races; and faith unites those whose forefathers were strangers.

Thus a young Frank, a *Poulain*, was accustomed from childhood
to meeting and living with the Occident in the Orient. The house or
citadel which he inhabited in the city was usually an oriental building
which had belonged to a Moslem before the Crusader conquest
and was very different from European buildings and fortifications.
Timber, the most common building material in the West, was almost
unknown in the Holy Land. Stone was the common building material
used in both the cities and villages. It was usually quarried not far from
the cities themselves, like the stone cut out of the slopes of Mount
Carmel for Caesarea, those of Chastel Pèlerin dug out of the nearby
ridge which blocked the eastward-moving dunes, or the lovely, pink-
coloured stone brought to Jerusalem from Anathot.

Two- and three-storey stone houses were the normal type of habitat,
but even five-storey houses were not unknown. Their flat roofs, often
dotted with potted palms or evergreen trees and shrubs, were a place
to enjoy the cool breezes after the hot sun had set. Inside, the thick
walls preserved warmth in the winter, when the temperature in places
like Jerusalem and Safed, as well as in the mountains east of Acre,
Tripoli and Antioch, descended to the freezing point. In the summer,
the walls and narrow windows kept the rooms cool, even during the
scorching days of the *hamsin*, the Levantine first-cousin of the *sirocco*.
The ceilings were very high, and the slightly pointed arches added to
the feeling of height in the atmosphere, for the narrow windows

restricted the entrance of light as well as heat. The windows were not boarded up by planks or covered with parchment, but glistened with locally fabricated glass. Pure, transparent glass was rather rare, but green- or blue-tinted, semi-opaque glass enclosing air bubbles was used, unless one preferred stained glass.

The ground-floor facade of Eastern houses was usually a solid wall except for the entrance-way. The windows on the upper floors let in some light, but basically the house opened onto the inner courtyard, where the precious, life-giving well, stored rain water or, in some places, a pit connected to one of the ancient aqueducts was normally situated. In some courtyards, as we know from a description of a marvellous Crusader palace in Beirut, a fountain cooled the air and its water-jets fell back into a mosaic-paved pool.

In some houses the staircase was located outside the building, allowing access from the street to each floor. The houses of the wealthy often had a kind of out-building composed of canvas – or plank – covered arches to protect the entrance from sun and rain, like the elaborate awnings in our luxury hotels. The shafts of the arches had holes drilled into them so that horses could be tethered.

The interiors of the better-endowed houses were decorated with mosaics of exquisite Byzantine-Moslem craftsmanship. In addition, rugs, draperies or tapestries covered the walls. Mosaics were an integral part of interior decoration and often displayed geometric designs, flowers and animals. In wealthier households, the ceiling arches may have rested on sculpted consoles, or a display of archvaults and simple arches might have added to the decor. Furniture was far more elaborate than that found in Europe. At their best, tables and chairs and the legs and posts of beds were of wood carved in lace-like patterns of bas-reliefs or small sculptures of flowers or human or animal heads. The chairs often looked like a rounded letter x, their upper part serving as a seat with handles. Oblong, cylindrical cushions covered with silk or samite that ended off in tassels were added for comfort. Mother of pearl, which became the glory of Bethlehem's craftsmanship, may already have been used in furniture decoration, as it was in some of the mosaics. Each noble household or ecclesiastical institution had a box-like writing table with accompanying chair. The writing was done on the inclined top, whereas the ink-pots, colours, quills and other paraphernalia of the scriptorium were kept on the table's lower shelves.

Kitchen utensils and tableware varied with the strata of society.

Cooking was done in large earthenware pots in open ovens. Those preserved in several Crusader sites are huge pits over which meat could have been broiled or pots suspended or the pit was covered by a special iron grid to hold the pots and pans. Spoons and knives were the basic table utensils, the first normally of wood, the latter of iron or steel. One often used his dagger as a table knife (these sometimes had ornate handles of ivory or carved wood and blades of the famous Indian steel), although metal utensils were often imported from Europe. In noble households the younger squires or pages served the meal; but when the family was receiving honoured guests, the younger sons of the family would sometimes perform this duty. The carved meat was transferred on slices of round bread, which served as plates and sauce-sponges, or the bread was placed on earthenware plates which were often glazed and decorated with designs. The most common glazed crockery was a basic dark colour covered with geometrical designs of brown, green and yellow glaze. Sometimes these decorations were Christian symbols – such as crosses, fish, tiaras, mitres – but heads of animals, legendary griffons and the like were also used. The most elaborate plates would have drawings of knights or riders on their mounts.

Metal plates and goblets were part of the decor of the house. Some were purely ornamental, such as large, copper-brimmed plates engraved with verses or even scenes from the Scriptures. These seem to have been imported from Europe; but such decorative or ceremonial crockery as that on which the Crusader king's meal was served in the Mosque of al-Aqsa after the coronation must have been of precious metal designed and engraved in Syria and Palestine. Metal cups and goblets were in common use. Some were inlaid, usually with silver, in the lovely patterns of the oriental arabesque. The Arabic inscriptions which praised Allah were no impediment to their use among Christians, though they might have been used for wine-drinking (which was certainly not what their artisan-creator intended). Whereas metal cups and goblets were also in common use in Europe, glassware was far more common in the Orient. Some examples of glasses painted with scenes and inscriptions, probably made in Tyre, display excellent form and exquisite decorations. One bears the heraldic sign of its owner, which must have been a common custom.

The oriental house and its interior decoration found their complement in the cuisine. Whatever gastronomical tradition had been imported from Europe, it could hardly compete with the local menu. Not only was oriental cuisine better adapted to the local climatic conditions, but the tantalizing spices and their use in meat, fish and sauces easily got the upper hand in competition with the abundant but rather plain dishes known to the Europeans. The oriental servants, like vendors in streets and bazaars, had no difficulty introducing their specialities into both noble and lower households. We even know about Crusader old-timers who boasted about their Egyptian cuisine, as one would boast today of having a cook with a *cordon bleu*.

Fashion and dresses also left their mark on Crusader society, but in this sphere the Franks limited their adoption. The Frank was ready to take advantage of the sumptuous textiles of the Near or Far East. Textiles which in Europe could have been found in royal and princely households only or occasionally among the ceremonial wardrobe of prelates were within the range of people of even mediocre means in the Orient. Silk, taffeta, brocade, cotton, wool and gossamer muslins were all worn by the Franks and their ladies, but they resisted the adoption of oriental style. One would wear oriental fabrics, but the cut of the dresses remained European. A Frank never wore any oriental garb, at least not in public. Sometimes he would wind a short shawl or mantle over his helmet as protection against the sun's strong rays; he might even use a white cloak, as did the Orientals and members of the military orders. But his vestments were basically European and changed with European fashions. Articles of clothing which could not be found in the kingdom, like berets, were imported from Europe. And the Franks' sense of ethnic identity went so far that they prohibited non-Franks from wearing European-style garments. This keeping to the *mores Francorum* was also expressed by the resistance to the oriental custom of growing beards. Whereas the participants of the First Crusade were bearded, as was the custom in their homelands, when beards went out of fashion in Europe two generations later (middle of the twelfth century), the Franks in the Holy Land followed suit, and their clean-shaven faces and shoulder-length hair became as much a clearly distinguishable mark of their identity as the object of oriental disgust and ridicule.

Climate and environment had their influence in the realm of hygiene and cosmetics. A nineteenth-century historian described medieval

Europe as a society which had forgone washing for a thousand years. This description certainly did not apply to the Franks in the East. Soap was produced locally and may even have been exported. The partiality of the *Poulains* for baths earned them the charge of the vice of 'luxury'. The austere Bernard of Clairvaux pointed out with pride that his protégés, the Templars, had no use for baths! Fifty years later, James of Vitry, the bishop of Acre, preached against this unholy institution which contaminated mores. He even hinted at some unsavoury goings on among the ladies of the Crusader upper class. The Genoese even allowed common bathing (albeit segregated by sex) in their *balneum* in Acre. Whatever the custom, Europeans who visited the kingdom returned to Europe with the impression that an effeminate society had succeeded the heroes of the First Crusade, who had since become legendary paragons of all chivalrous virtues. Today, one would probably describe such behaviour as subtlety, finesse or epicurean, but things looked different to the European newcomer. James of Vitry was rather vehement in his denunciation: 'They were brought up in luxury, soft and effeminate, more used to baths than battles, addicted to unclean and riotous living, clad like women in soft robes. Beneath the heavy hand of the furious prelate, one detects a mode of life which a disgruntled contemporary observer would label as Levantine:

They have so learned to disguise their meaning in cunning speeches, covered and bedecked with leaves, but no fruit, like barren willow-trees, that those who do not know them thoroughly by experience can scarcely understand their reservations and tricks of speech or avoid being deceived by them. They are suspicious and jealous of their wives, whom they lock up in close prison and guard in such strict and careful custody that even their brethren and nearest relatives can scarcely approach them; while they forbid them so utterly to attend churches, processions, the wholesome preaching of God's Word and other matters appertaining to their salvation, that they scarce suffer them to go to church once a year; howbeit some husbands allow their wives to go out to the bath three times a week, under strict guard.

As to Crusader womenfolk:

But the more strictly the *Pullani* lock up their wives, the more do they by a thousand arts and endless contrivances struggle and try to find their way out. They are wondrously and beyond belief learned in witchcraft and wickednesses innumerable, which they are taught by the Syrian women.

above Riding, tournaments and hunting were the pastimes of the Crusader nobility. This illumination from a 13th-century French history of the Crusades shows a riding party of lay and ecclesiastical pilgrims and crusaders (46)

left Among the new vistas of the Orient, the Roman Church remained permanent and immutable. This bishop's staff, used by a Crusader prelate, was imported from Europe (47)

left The grimness of castles enlivened. A keystone from the Teutonic knights' castle of Montfort in Galilee (48)

opposite The autonomous quarters of the mercantile communes fortified themselves against both neighbor and foe. The guard room of a Venetian corner tower in Acre is a remnant of 'Little Italy in the Holy Land' (49)

below European masons and sculptors mingled with oriental craftsmen in the Holy Land. Tomb engravers at work (50)

Hunting with falcons and cheetahs was a popular pastime of Mameluk nobles.
A hunting scene from a 14th-century Mameluk brass vessel inlaid with silver

(51)

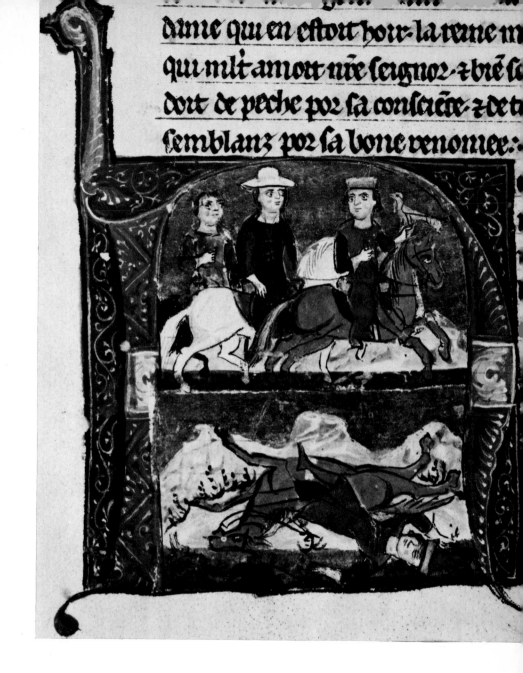

dame qui en estoit hoir · la reine m
qui mlt amoit nre seignor · z bie s
doit de peche por sa conscere · z de t
semblanz por sa bone renomee ·:

King Amalric shown during a fatal hunting party in this 13th-century
Crusader illuminated manuscript from Acre (52)

above A Crusader princess with a lady-in-waiting and an armoured knight (53)
below, *left* Crusader daily costume from a Crusader stele at Bethphage (54)
below, *right* Master Jacob de Laghini teaching the subtle art of reading (55)

above An elegant meal–oriental fashion (56)
below An elegant meal –Western fashion, showing a Crusader family at the
table, from an illuminated manuscript of the Book of Ruth (57)

above left A crusader swordsman (58). *right* A crusader lady (59). Both are
ceramics from Cyprus, 13th–14th century
below Musicians, from a 13th-century Crusader Bible (60)

Despite almost chronic warfare, the amenities of the Holy Land made life less grim than it was under the grey, northern skies of Europe. Houses, dress, encounters in street or market-place, the gossip and politics in the baths recalled Hellenistic cities. The Frankish knight who grew up in such surroundings, despite his speech and dress, was not French but a Near Eastern Frank. One can hardly agree with the accusation of cowardice; they were good fighters. And while not always good diplomats, thirteenth-century Crusader nobles were born politicians who loved to have a finger in every political pie and conspiracy, like the Renaissance Italians in their city-states.

The Frankish noble seldom lived in the countryside. Even the few nobles who had castles as centres of seignories would normally maintain a household in the city (usually in Jerusalem and in the thirteenth century in Acre or Tyre). Very few nobles lived in their manors. Basically they were a class of *rentiers* who collected the income from their rural estates and spent it in their urban residences. The countryside and its villages was a thing one lived off, supervised, but rarely inhabited. The squire-tenant or squire-serf relationship, typical in medieval Europe, was almost non-existent in the Orient. The steward or a similar official, often a scribe or *drugeman*, would supervise the village rents, though he seldom intervened in the work itself. The Crusader noble did not go into farming on his own, very seldom kept demesne land and was normally satisfied with the third or quarter of the village crops, which were usually well supplemented by income from urban taxation. As a matter of fact, a Crusader noble's visit to his rural possessions was rather exceptional. One went out to the countryside for hunting or fishing, but seldom for economic reasons. The amenities of country life, without its burdens, were supplied by the beautiful orchards, vineyards and olive groves which surrounded all the cities. Some nobles maintained a kind of cottage or similar structure in these 'suburbs' where they passed the hot summer days and cooler evenings in the company of others of their class, sometimes even Moslem nobles. From here they would pursue the chase for fox or boar or hunt with falcons. A good part of time was spent in riding and military exercises. Crusader nobles, like their Moslem antagonists, vied with each other over the beauty of their horses. A considerable amount of money was spent acquiring horses and bedecking them with trappings of finery, expensive materials and precious metals. Pasture lands around the cities were also parade grounds to display horses and horsemanship. During periods of peace, even Moslems would participate in such exercises. The crowning glory of the mounted noble was, naturally, the tournament, a mock battle of nobles or of single champions. On such occasions the ladies appeared on city or castle battlements to participate in that most-cherished of medieval shows. Here the young squire or the experienced knight could achieve prize and renown for prowess and military skill. The horses, arms and armour of the loser, often of considerable value, became the property of the winner. Still, it seems that tournaments, which were often connected with festivities, were rarer in the Crusader East than in contemporary Europe. Perhaps in a war-ridden country mock battles were too close to everyday, grim reality to exercise the attraction that was so strong in Europe, despite ecclesiastical pro-hibitions.

The major part of a noble's or knight's time was spent in his normal habitat, the city. A simple knight's time-table was regulated by duties of service in city garrison, manning the city's citadel, making the rounds of walls and towers or guarding the lord's palace. Higher nobility would spend a good deal of time in attendance on their overlord, often sitting in his court as councillors or judges. As councillors they would advise on matters put before them for deliberation; as judges they performed the feudal obligations judging their peers.

A short treatise entitled 'On the Four Ages of Men', written by a mid-thirteenth-century Frank and describing occupations fitting to each age, gives the impression that the Franks in the East were a noble, church-going society. Unfortunately, this picture clashes too strongly with other sources – albeit of ecclesiastical origin – which give a very different version of the nobles' behaviour. Whatever the truth, whether or not one really attended daily mass, there is no doubt that a noble would participate in the great church festivities which, in a city like Jerusalem, were not only religiously moving, but offered a rich pageantry to participant and spectator.

For other amusements and social contacts, one would meet friends at home, at the bath or even in a tavern. Chess – the king's game – was known, but dice was the most popular entertainment, and one ran the risk of losing both fortune and soul. Meals and drinking – heavy drinking – were part and parcel of entertainment, and many a tavern or private house had its quota of Western-style prostitutes or Eastern-style dancing girls, sometimes slaves of an oriental *souteneur*. Prostitution, common in all medieval cities and most accentuated in ports, was quite extensive in a port city like Acre, where the pope had to warn clergy about renting houses to prostitutes. We have a vivid description of this city, recorded by James of Vitry, who was bishop of Acre for some time:

Among the *Poulains* there is hardly one in a thousand who takes his marriage seriously. They do not regard fornication to be a deadly sin. From childhood they are pampered and wholly given to carnal pleasures, whereas they are not accustomed to hear God's work, which they lightly disregard. I found here foreigners who fled in despair from their native countries because of various horrible sins. These people, who have no fear of God, are corrupting the whole city by their nefarious deeds and pernicious examples.

Almost every day and every night people are openly or secretly murdered. At night men strangle their wives if they dislike them; women, using the ancient art of poison and potion, kill their husbands so as to be able to marry other men. There are in the city vendors of toxins and poisons, so that nobody can have confidence in anyone, and a man's foes shall be they of his own household.

And the city is full of brothels, and as the rent of the prostitutes is higher, not only laymen, but even clergymen, nay even monks, rent their houses all over the city to public harlots.

It is difficult to ascertain the degree of literacy among the Frankish nobility. It seems that the higher nobility was literate, and the rather few works written by them, as well as other testimonies, indicate that their level of literacy was equal to that of their European counterparts. We know of festivities where episodes from the Arthurian cycle, as well as the fabliaux popular in Europe were performed. But it is doubtful whether the same degree of literacy was common among the lower nobility. Likewise, we know very little about the nobility's intellectual interests. Very few seem to have been interested in the rich oriental heritage around them, and few mastered Arabic, the common language of the Orient and the key to its treasures. On the whole, this breed of Europeans in the East does not strike one as being bent on an intellectual adventure.

The general lack of intellectual interests is stressed by the fact that no scholarly or intellectual centre, no university of school was ever created in the Crusader colonies – and this in an age when all major European centres were dotted with colleges or universities. A man bent on acquiring a wider education went to Europe, as did the only historian of the kingdom, William, bishop of Tyre, a *Poulain*, who

easily ranks among the greatest historians in the Middle Ages. This
phenomenon in itself explains why the Crusader colonies never became
bridges between the Orient and Occident, despite the fact that for
two hundred years they were the outposts of Europe in the Eastern
Mediterranean.

Low-keyed involvement in the realm of thought and spirit had one
major exception: the particular interest of the nobility in the customary
laws of the kingdom, that is, feudal law as practised in Jerusalem and
Cyprus. The native nobility were its chief exponents, and although
it seems that they had some knowledge of Roman law – enough,
at least, to quote from it – the law of the kingdom was customary
medieval law. Their mastery of the subject was such that some of the
works of the Crusader jurists remained classics in European legal
literature, almost textbooks of feudal law, and were used and quoted
down to the French Revolution, when the new *Code* did away with
feudal law. In reading the treatises of Jean d'Ibelin or Philip of Novara,
one is impressed by the sheer joy of these jurists in dwelling upon the
minutiae of the law, its ramifications and possible applications – a type
of hair-splitting worthy of scholastic theologians. It seems that this
interest in law channeled all the intellectual energies of the Crusader
nobility. They learned law when still young by attending the meetings
of the royal or lordly court and were instructed in it by their elders.
One youngster was even taught the legal traditions of the country
during a military campaign. No less remarkable than the interest in
law *per se* is the fact that a law treatise was often written as a vademecum
on how to circumvent the law, an exercise in subtleties which was
concerned less with the pursuit of justice than with the way to win a
case! Such activities hardly seem to befit the noble knight, the worthy
successor of the gathering at the Round Table or of the companions of
Roland. One could say that if the Crusader nobility was not influenced
by latent germs of Greek philosophy, it at least attained Levantine
versatility. But this may be a rather harsh judgement if one realises that
this study of law was linked with the nobility's elementary urge to
safeguard its 'franchises and liberties', which they viewed as identical
with the constitutional freedom of the kingdom.

If Frankish nobility could usually trace their origin to a noble
house in their European homeland – though not to the famous
houses of Christendom – the burgesses, despite their title, were hardly
descendants of European burghers or city dwellers. The lower strata

of Frankish population was predominantly of peasant stock, villeins and serfs. They had left Europe either with one of the crusades or as part of a wave of migration. And it was this strata of society which made up the majority of the Frankish population. The transition from their basically rural life-style to the mastery of urban occupations was not an easy one. The native craftsmen, oriental Christians or Moslems, could offer far superior products which were better adapted to local needs and were certainly more elegant than anything usually produced in the manorial worksheds of Europe. The burgesses, however, had the advantage of being able to produce goods according to European tastes and create fashions more easily acceptable to the new settlers. They also enjoyed the fact that the new immigrants preferred their own kin; but this advantage quickly disappeared – as it always does – in the face of the competitive prices of local talent.

It was this strata of immigrants which made up the new society's middle class of craftsmen and merchants, occupations which were seldom distinct. They filled the demand for tailors, shoemakers, goldsmiths, carpenters, smiths, millers, cooks, bakers, confectioners, and candle-makers. In the ports and anchorage places, the new profession of catering, to assure ships provisions for the three-week voyage to Europe, developed. And other new occupations appeared, like the muleteers and camel-drivers; porters of water; spice, incense and perfume vendors; and, naturally, guides, suppliers of holy relics, and publicans. The latter were notorious throughout Christendom. Pilgrim and immigrant alike constantly complained of being cheated. Some taverns which served as hostelries in the ports and in centres of pilgrimage were often also bawdy houses. It was here that prostituion and dice games flourished to the outrage of those who were bent on penitence and spirituality.

On another plane, the burgesses filled the ranks of the kingdom's lower officialdom, whether in the city or in the lordship's rural administration. Some acquired enough Arabic to serve as dragomans; others, more literate, filled the office of scribes or petition-writers. We can visualise them squatting near the lord's or bishop's dwellings, with their portable tables, ink-pots, quills and strips of parchment, penning (for remuneration) the humble requests of the simple people. Then there were the administrative tasks proper. Both lordly and ecclesiastical institutions needed stewards to run their estates and their revenues, assure provisions for their households and to supervise their servants.

At the gates of cities and entrances to the ports, a swarm of scribes, customs and tax collectors performed these duties in the din of haggling and recriminations.

The Crusader burgesses in the triple bazaars of Jerusalem or the *souks* of Antioch, Tripoli and Acre rented their nooks, stalls and benches from the city lord or an ecclesiastical institution. Here they sold their wares, the agricultural yield of their gardens and orchards or products purchased in the countryside to be resold to the city dwellers. Another typical burgess occupation was that of the money-changer. It was often connected with lending money and was the nearest the Frankish burgess ever came to the realm of high finance. Serious activities in high finance were beyond his reach because historical circumstances during the earliest period of conquest made the field a *de facto* monopoly of the Italian (later also Provençal and Catalan) merchants.

Beginning with the First Crusade, but especially during the following first decade of the kingdom, when the crusaders were fighting the Moslem powers from Cilicia to the Red Sea, the fleets of Venice, Pisa and Genoa – the great European emporia – were instrumental in the conquest of the maritime cities of Syria, Lebanon and the Holy Land. The Italians, whose participation in the Crusades was motivated by a mixture of religious ideals and material calculations, asked to be remunerated for their services. The pious declaration that they sailed to the East to fight the Holy War and in the service of Christianity did not prevent them from assuring themselves a share in the conquest – not only the immediate, tangible booty (which was not negligible), but more permanent gains in the form of streets or quarters in the cities, exemptions from tax and customs and privileges of immunity and autonomy in ruling their nationals and managing their possessions. Thus every major Frankish city in the Levant – and with the exception of Jerusalem, all of them were maritime cities – had at least one, but usually several streets or quarters which belonged to the various Italian communes. The Italians were the third distinctive class among the Franks (along with the nobles and burgesses), and their presence added to the variety of nations and to the Babel of languages.

The Italian settlements were not created immediately after the conquest. Few merchants settled during the early years of the kingdom, but the administrative nucleus sent from the Italian metropolis to safeguard its rights and privileges was a permanent fixture even then. It represented a foothold, but its future depended on the ability to use possessions in Antioch, Tyre or Acre as a basis for business. Realities never matched their expectations because even the great Crusader cities were not centres of production, or at least could not compare with Constantinople or Alexandria. Neither were they outlets for a rich hinterland. Consequently, European commerce could not forgo direct contacts with such Moslem or Byzantine centres. Nonetheless, the privileged position of the communes in the Crusader establishments counter-balanced the obvious economic handicaps. For example, the customs exemptions enjoyed by the communes made the Crusader centres an ideal depot for merchandise imported from the Moslem hinterland – like medieval free ports on the Mediterranean. With the growing volume of trade and more daring penetration of the Moslem hinterland, Italian merchants who had used the Crusader ports only as way-stations began to prolong their stay in the Levant, and fairly sizeable Italian-merchant settlements were founded in all the major ports of the Crusader establishments in the East.

The communes, as such settlements were called, were a strange world – sort of colonies within colonies. A minority surrounded by a French-speaking majority, the Italians used and abused the 'foreign language', as did everyone else, in their contacts with their fellow Franks. But inside their quarters, in the precincts of the '*fondaco*', one was transported to beloved Italy. Once Byzantine or Moslem merchandise was acquired, business was often transacted between the Italian merchants themselves. Here each spoke his peculiar dialect of Venetian, Tuscan or Ligurian. Notaries wrote Latin, or sometimes thirteenth-century French, but thought in Italian. The Italians had all the conditions to preserve their identity. The commune overlord was not only of the quarter but also proprietor of all real estate within it. Large and often resplendent buildings – once the lodgings of a Moslem, Byzantine or Turkish governor or official – or houses which belonged to the Moslem merchant aristocracy of the city became *palazzi* in the Italian inventories and were taken over by the commune's administration. Buildings too large to serve any practical needs were divided into *camerae* (rooms rented for limited periods) and *magazini* (rooms to store merchandise). They often stood empty for the greater part of the year, but filled to overflowing when a *stola*, (fleet of ships) arrived from Europe at around Easter time.

The main street or square of the quarter became the market-place, and the houses which surrounded it usually contained shops, stalls and magazines where the oriental merchandise waiting to be exported to Europe or imported European merchandise waiting for buyers were deposited. The merchants lodged in the upper floors. Taverns and hostelries catering to the Italian palate were to be found everywhere. In addition, *banci* (benches) were set up by money-changers and vendors of perishable foodstuffs. Besides shops and magazines, a market-place and usually a vaulted bazaar, each quarter had its bakeries, ovens and baths. Some Italian banking families even saw fit to open subsidiaries in the Crusader cities, and big business, still being family business, sent members of the trading clans to Palestine.

The center of the quarter was the *palazzo* of the commune, which housed its administration. It housed the *vicomte* or consul, the governor sent from the mother-city. Supported by a council, he represented the commune's interest vis-à-vis the city's lord, ruler or king and was responsible for the management of the commune's possessions and privileges in the city. The notaries attached to him would draft agreements between merchants and marriage contracts; the jurors would sit in judgement or arbitration in cases regarding their own nationals, but in some cases they would also judge other inhabitants of the quarter. Crimes punishable by death, such as homicide or rape, were sometimes excepted from this system, and the guardians of peace – beadles or sergeants – would arrest the accused and turn him over to the seigniorial authorities. There was always some bickering in such cases as the Italians were naturally reluctant to hand over one of their own to external jurisdiction. The law of the communal courts was not that of the kingdom but that of the Italian mother-city. The proceedings were held in the merchants' native language, the procedure was familiar from homeland and the judgement was made by their peers. The head of the commune had his contingent of scribes and sergeants. The first were responsible for the inventory of the commune's property and for collecting rents, which were duly registered in '*quaterna*' (account books) and guarded in the community chest. The town crier and sergeants announced the ordinances of the commune's council and supervised their execution. Time and again ordinances prohibiting prostitution and gambling were issued, but in such communities of travelling salesmen, they were of doubtful effect.

opposite View of the 12th-century Crusader castle of Belvoir, a magnificent observation point overlooking the Jordan Valley

Though the mother-cities might have drawn some direct financial profits from these colonies, their main income from the Levant came indirectly by taxing those merchants in Italy who prospered from the Levantine trade. But such assets often became a liability. The communes were in open competition on both sea and land. They fought each other for privileges, but even more important was the fact that they transferred Italian-mainland rivalries to the emporia of the Levant. For more than a generation during the thirteenth century, any encounter between the respective Italian fleets on the open sea ended in battle or piracy, while the walls of Acre and Tyre were resounding with the thud of stone projectiles. The communal quarters entrenched themselves within a girdle of walls flanked by towers when neighbouring quarters became enemy territory. In such circumstances the merchant became as much a warrior as every sailor was a marine. Moreover, ships and reinforcements sent from Italy added the horrors of maritime blockade to the fratricidal fighting inside the city walls. Towers and walls were often breached, houses burnt and destroyed and a column or crier's stone carried away in triumph to the mother-city to adorn the main *piazza*. Thus the cities of the Levant often became a miniature projection of life in Italy itself.

The level of literacy among the Italians was certainly higher than that of the average Frank. This was true in Europe as well, but the contrast was even more accentuated in the milieu of international merchants. Correspondence and accounts were part of everyday business. Knowledge of geography and economy was surprisingly developed if we are to judge by the extant merchants' manuals or the new invention, the *portolani* (maritime charts), which facilitated navigation. Whereas war resulted in a limited knowledge of the enemy and his land, commerce created an all-embracing web of links from Scandinavia to Sahara, from Spain to Mesopotamia and, by the middle of the thirteenth century, over Persia to India and China. The Italians possessed not only an academic knowledge of lands and countries, but a practical knowledge of the routes over mountain, valley, desert, river and sea. They also developed a detailed familiarity with means of production, merchandise to be bought or wares to be sold, and the taxes and customs in ports with strange-sounding names, which in European parlance became even stranger and were sometimes distorted beyond recognition. They also mastered knowledge of currencies, their metallic value and exchange rates around the world.

The communal quarters became often a repository of such knowledge, which was transmitted orally, then recorded and finally compiled into manuals, a '*Pratica della mercatura*', for the instruction, if not necessarily the edification, of a new generation of apprentices in the art of buying, selling, loans and financing. A young Italian might well be sent to Syria, Armenia or Constantinople for his apprenticeship. He might then settle in one of these places and strike out on his own. If marriage did not appear in the offing in the Levant or his suitorship was not crowned with success, he might return to his homeland in search of a bride and a dowry, which was usually counted in imperishable spices like pepper or in precious stones. In time, some Italian families only loosely linked with their homeland struck roots in the East and became firmly established there. From stall to market, from bench to magazine, their life was spent among their own kin. Even the church in the quarter was only partially tied to the local ecclesiastical hierarchy and depended on the cathedral in the homeland. The priest and his acolytes were sent from Venice, Genoa or Pisa. The Italian or Provençal spoke to the priest in his native venacular and the Sunday sermon was delivered in a language he understood.

Though the inhabitants of the communal quarters were supposedly citizens of the Crusader kingdom, in reality they remained citizens of their European metropolis. Despite a thousand links with France, no Frank regarded himself as French, but the members of the communes never abandoned their original identity. Settling together helped to preserve this identity, but there were also material reasons for clinging to one's national group. A hundred and even two hundred years after the establishment of the kingdom, the Italians still enjoyed the privileges of those who had participated in the conquest of the country. Though one could justify their rights to real estate (for, after all, all Frankish property resulted from the conquests during the first decade of the kingdom), it was rather strange, to say the least, that they should continue to enjoy the exemption from taxes and customs acquired eight or ten generations earlier. Their privileged position made any competition with the local Franks, who paid full customs, simply unthinkable. No doubt this situation was galling, as it was hardly possible to explain why the Italians should enjoy a privileged position without rendering any visible service to the kingdom.

Time and again the rulers of the kingdom tried to curtail what appeared to be exorbitant privileges. The communes fought back by mobilising the papacy, which had a clear interest in having the powerful maritime cities as its allies. The pontiffs fulminated against the perjury of the kings, threatening them with anathema; and the Crusader rulers almost always yielded to pressure. The Genoese, with more acumen than tact, inscribed the tenor of their privileges in golden letters on a column and then erected it in the Church of the Holy Sepulchre! The only way of curtailing the communes' privileges was by removing high justice from the hands of the communes and enforcing the prohibition against selling them fiefs or lands held by burgage tenure. But even when employing such measures, the royal opposition was only partially successful, as mixed marriages brought the Italians the lands of heiresses and their feudal or burgage possessions.

The degree to which the settlers of Italian origin mixed with the local Franks is rather difficult to ascertain. We know of Italians who looked for brides in Europe, but marriages with the local Frankish population were common. A Frankish family may well have seen it as advantageous to marry off their daughters to the Italian and Provençal merchants. Such a union was not considered a *mésalliance*, and it normally meant a step up on the social and economic ladder. The story of the wealthy merchant from Pisa who married a member of the Frankish aristocracy in Tripoli must have made the rounds of Oriental *souks*. To receive the permission to marry the young lady, the merchant paid to the maiden's noble warden her weight in gold! A hundred and twenty or so pounds of pure gold could weigh down many barriers.

Some other families entered Frankish life not through marriage but through feudal positions. A Genoese family like the Embriaci, to whom the commune rented its property in the city of Gebal, severed its links with the mother-city and became part and parcel of the Frankish aristocracy. That they continued to favour their compatriots in the city, however, was to be expected. On a lower level, Italian families entered the Frankish *bourgeoisie* through marriage, which we know from documentation of the legal bickering over whether the marriage contract should follow local or Italian custom. Whatever the degree of assimilation through marriage, the Italians remained a power unto themselves, maintaining the customs, language and institution of the Rialto or Porto Vecchio in the Holy Land.

7

The Romance of Chivalry and the Military Orders

Chivalry is the most spectacular and perhaps even the most sublime expression of the spirit of the Middle Ages. No virtues were more extolled, exploits more retold, images more impressive than those of the noble knight. The word evokes a whole world, a way of life, system of upbringing, set of attitudes and rules of behaviour, as well as material surroundings – the manor-house, the stronghold, castle and citadel. The ethos of chivalry was paramount for more than three hundred years, and there is hardly any other single ideal in Western culture, with the exception of Universal Peace, which could rival its vitality over so long a period of time. Even when chivalry disappeared as a distinctive class ideology, its ideals remained. And while some became fossilised and turned into soulless rites, others ended in pompous and artificial associations, still others were metamorphosed into pyramids of symbols which collapsed under their own weight, chivalry nonetheless survived in the concept of the gentleman, in the rites – even sentiments – of courting and in rules of behaviour appropriate to a civilised society. When chivalry shed its external trappings and lost its standing as the monopolistic attribute of the ruling class, it remained a living force which permeated society at large.

Chivalry, which can best be described as the system of ideals of the hereditary, warrior class of the Middle Ages, was no more created by the Crusades than the Crusades were the product of chivalry. Yet going on a crusade became part of the lofty ideals of knighthood.

Chivalry's formalised expression, that is rules of behaviour, existed many centuries before they were recorded and codified. As a matter of fact, when the codification began at the turn of the fourteenth century, the institution of chivalry was already approaching its decadence. But literary expressions of chivalry's ideals, in the form of legends centred on the noble Christian hero, were contemporary with the classical period of the Crusades (i.e., the twelfth and thirteenth centuries). Moreover, one of the most striking manifestations of the ideals of chivalry, the development of the military orders, was also one of the most original creations of the Crusades and of the Latin establishments in the East.

The unwritten code of behaviour of the upper stratum of medieval society (i.e., the warrior class) drew upon ancient Germanic sources which were common to almost all warrior classes in tribal society. It was a code praising and sanctioning the virtues of the brave and the loyal. Bravery, daring and great feats of arms were the *leitmotif* of the early Germanic – continental as well as Anglo-Saxon – epics. But even at this early stage, physical strength and prowess, skill in arms and ruse in battle were accompanied by the demand for loyalty and solidarity. Loyalty to the chieftain, warlord or battle leader and solidarity with comrades in arms were the normative rules of the warrior. Some of these characteristics can be traced back some three hundred years before the Germanic invasions in Tacitus's description of the turbulent tribes of Germany. The Germanic invasions, the great migrations which changed the map of the civilised world at the dawn of the Middle Ages, served to strengthen and elaborate the ideals of the ferocious Germanic warrior. Charismatic leadership disappeared during the invasions, but the ideals remained. The king's or leader's bodyguard might have been the repository of these ideals, but they were not a monopoly of a class, as the noble class which came into being under the Merovingians and early Carolingians was not hereditary but a nobility of service to king and great lord.

It was only during the ninth and, even more so, tenth centuries that war became an attribute of a particular class and was thus divorced from the great mass of the common people. From that time the ideals of the warrior were limited to an élite which became almost universally hereditary at the beginning of the eleventh century. Heredity gave rise to new elements during the formative age of knighthood's ideals. Pride in the deeds of one's ancestors created the concept of family tradition and the legend of the noble dynasty. And while a commoner could still enter the nobility by proving himself in an act of bravery, such as instance of social mobility was certainly the exception and not the rule. The nobility itself, independent of the accompanying development of the feudal system, was hierarchically structured, its apex being the territorial prince or king. Lesser and lower nobility, down to the base of the pyramid, expressed their ideals through loyalty to the local ruling dynasty, a sentiment far stronger than the mediated loyalty to the rising feudal monarchies. The new structure of society and the ideals of its warrior élite found their institutional expression in vassaldom and in the lord-vassal relationship. This became the emotional mortar which assured cohesion in a turbulent world.

Though fighting and hunting were the usual occupation and pastime of the nobility, periods of peace occasioned social encounters beyond those of the armed host or hunting group. It was at these gatherings – often festive, even if they were convened to transact business – at the lord's court or castle that armour was exchanged for softer vestments of linen or sometimes even expensive silks and brocades brought from the East by Italian merchants. In this new milieu, new values began to develop, while not supplanting the existing ones. The most symptomatic expression of this evolution was the appearance of women in the castle hall not as servants or onlookers, but very often as centre of social life and the focus of the noble household.

The great noble family – called the *lignage* to stress the importance of origin – became the primary framework of a vassal's life. Even if the vassals were not blood-relations, they were considered part of the *lignage* and paternal relations were added to those based on social loyalty. The loyalty of the former warrior group remained undisputed and undivided, but it now meant something more; it created a 'sense of belonging'. One gave of himself, his family, property, faculties and emotions. Paternal as the relations might have been, they did not imply condescension, because the total engagement – the 'commendation', as it was called – was mutual. 'The lord owes to his man as much as the man owes to his lord' – except for reverence – was the expression commonly employed to define the relations. This was a far more subtle and deep-reaching relationship than that of the preceding age. It reflected a new type of human relations, that of the great feudal family, in which one assumed responsibility for the welfare of others not only at critical moments on the battlefield.

Though deeply anchored in the barbarian past, this new form of relations soon created its own constellation of values and modes of behaviour. The court gathering created courtesy, manners befitting the assembly and the presence of womenfolk, now ladies. Borrowing from the feudal system, they became *dominae*, *les dames*. They adorned the meetings at court, presided at banquets and added lustre to the festivals. Soon they played a major role in the most spectacular expression of chivalry, the tournament. Thus a new realm of behaviour, sensibilities and tastes came into being in the castle halls of medieval Europe. The gloomy, dark halls, illuminated by torches which cast menacing shadows on the gargantuan meals of the warriors, became filled with light and laughter. The wandering singer and rhymester, who until now sang of the valour and armed skill of heroes, their titanic fights and gross appetites, introduced new themes into his repertory. He sang of life and love, of nature and youth. The singer of the heroic epic became the minstrel, troubadour, the minnesinger. The heroic, haughty figure of the barbarian hero was mollified, and lofty feelings, the sublime in love and devotion, were now shared by the feudal lord and the lord of the heart.

At the turn of the eleventh century, even the images of war and fighting were metamorphosed. The deeds of the Nibelungs, the exploits of Beowulf, the battles of chieftains and tribal war lords took on now a new meaning that foreshadowed the spirit of the Crusades. Fighting was channelled; the permanent and chaotic war of neighbour against neighbour, foes almost by definition, was curbed by a new ideology, according to which one was not supposed to fight a Christian neighbour or attack for private vengeance and glory. The real turnabout, however, was that fighting was henceforth not only tolerated, but even sanctioned and encouraged if the aim was moral. Following the precepts of the Scriptures, the Church had been opposed to any kind of bloodshed. Though since the time of St Augustine fighting had found some justification in the notions of self-defence or a just war, the Church shunned military activities on principle. But its ideals were of little or no avail when the barbarians invaded the Roman Empire and contesting tribes butchered each other. Even when Europe regained a sense of stability under Charlemagne, the Church could do no more than reiterate its negative attitude towards bloodshed. In the ninth century, the pope appealed to Christian warriors to defend Rome against the threat of Moslem infidels, who captured the Mediterranean and established bridgeheads on the European mainland from Spain through France to Sicily. But this was an exceptional situation, and the Church did not change its general stand. In the eleventh century it even initiated popular movements to curb the excesses of the nobility. At about the same time, however, some three generations before the First Crusade, a marked change took place in the attitude of the Church, or at least of some of its representatives. This was not the first nor the last time the Church resigned itself to legitimatising an existing situation. It was ready to compromise and accept the standing order of society, though it dictated its own conditions of partial capitulation. The Church was ready to sanction war and warrior if it could determine their motivations and aims.

In the new perspective, the fighting man, the 'man of blood', was entrusted with a social function: to defend the poor, widows and orphans. Falling back on biblical precepts, the Church conceded that fighting be permitted for a just cause, the protection of the weak against the strong aggressor. Thus the primeval urge to fight would be channelled and made socially useful. When applied to existing conditions, this was a revolutionary idea. Suddenly the warriors' boundless energies, unbridled tempers and bloodthirst were curbed, and the spoilers and depredators of yesterday were metamorphosed into guardians of society. While the order of clerics assured the goodwill of Providence and preached basic morals to a half-barbarian society, the warrior class became an 'order' of society whose function was to protect the non-combattant and the weak. The wielding of arms was neither an end in itself nor an independent source of pride. It became a means to an end, and its righteousness was directly related to its use for a worthy cause.

It seems that the warrior class was as ready to face the challenge as the Church to raise it. The result was a metamorphosis of the fighting man. The soldier, the Roman '*miles*', had long since become a class designation reserved for the élite mounted warriors. (Those who fought on foot, the '*pedites*', did not warrant the title.) Thus in the early Middle Ages '*miles*' really meant a rider, *chevalier* or *Ritter*, as he might be designated by Anglo-Saxons, French or Germans, respectively. During the eleventh century a new expression was coined: '*Miles Christianus*', a Christian knight, a combination of Christian morality and Germanic warfare. The new knightly Christian ideology easily found its way into the repertory of medieval poets. Retribution for evil acts, the protection of the weak and the defence of the lady's honour and chastity became the subject matter of twelfth- and thirteenth-century poetry and found their most sublime literary expression in the romances of chivalry. Whatever their origin, whatever the names of their heroes or authors, all the romances celebrated the same ideals because European chivalry was not restricted to any given nation; it was a kind of an

blectecs on leur droit
amenuisie en fondant
les teuant dites chofes
en leur droitures defus
dites. li teniort roys or
tena cntiers les efglules
et tres latir de faint cor
nille de compiegne qui pu

tion de ces efglules ain
li que il donna .c. luures
de parifis pour les droi
tures teuant dites. Et
fine le .xvij. chapit.
et commence le .xix.
qui eft de fa debonai
re demence.

oueur et de
bonnaurete
nauenent

a nul tome tant com
me a prince. Et pour te
li tenior faint loys fu

The virtues of the ideal Christian knight: devotion, bravery and gallantry. St Louis, in the midst of battle, saves a dark-skinned lady and her child. From an illuminated biography of St Louis by Guillaume de Saint Pathus (61)

above The life of the Christian knight.
In the upper panel, a castle manned by
vassals. A garrison of mailed knights
and provisions enter the castle, while
centaurs blow trumpets from the
battlements. In the lower panel, a
tournament (62)

right A didactic inscription from the
castle of Crac des Chevaliers: 'Have
riches / have wisdom / have beauty. /
It is pride / which contaminates /
everything it touches' (63)

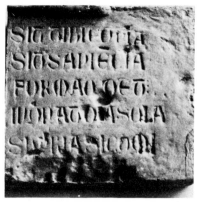

above Leisure in a princely household. Lord and lady playing chess attended by a lady-in-waiting and a young squire with a falcon (64)

left The Christian knight fought for the True Faith, the glory of God and the safety of Christendom. The destruction of idols and the annihilation of idolatry by the Maccabees, from a 13th-century illuminated Crusader manuscript (65)

The reunion. The husband, lost in a crusade, returns after many years in Moslem captivity. A 12th-century statue from the Eglise des Cordeliers in Nancy (66)

above The military orders, guardians of pilgrims and holy shrines, became the mainstay of the kingdom's military might. A fresco from the Templar church at Cressac, 13th-century (67)

left The care of the sick and poor was the province of the Hospitallers. A hospital scene from an early 13th-century Spanish manuscript showing a bishop exorcising the devil (68)

left A knight of the Order of Saint John (69)

opposite The magnificent refectory of the Hospitaller palace in Acre. Below the column is a secret passage connecting the refectory with the order's compound (70)

below, *left* The Stables of Solomon, beneath the Mosque of al-Aqsa, were used by the Templars' garrison (71)

below The Templars' compound in Jerusalem. The former Mosque of al-Aqsa was ceded to the knights by the kings of Jerusalem (72)

A scribe at work as depicted in a 13th-century illuminated Bible (73)

international brotherhood of the hereditary nobility, and it allowed a knight to feel at home in any court of Christendom. Wars were not eliminated, but fighting followed mutually accepted rules. Above all, however, chivalry implied a society of men linked by the feeling of belonging to a common class, living according to common patterns of behaviour and sharing a dedication to common goals and ideals.

Soon the hero of the chivalric romances would be leaving his home-land to fulfil the obligations incumbent upon a member of his class. He would be fighting blood-thirsty giants and vicious dragons, saving chaste maidens in distress and the lives of the weak. But he would also travel far and wide and perform feats of bravery in his search for the fabulous Holy Grail, the bowl which received the holy blood of the Saviour on the Cross. Blanchefleur and Isolde, Perceval and Tristan, King Arthur, Gawain, Lancelot and many more would densely populate the newly discovered world of experience: adventure, love, unknown lands and the pursuit of unattainable goals. The dim halls of the castles were replaced by the spring fields and flowers, streams and joyous meetings.

The Crusades had a marked influence on the development of the ideals of chivalry. They provided the first opportunity for knights throughout Christendom to come together bent on a common goal. The Crusades fostered the feeling of an international Christian brother-hood-in-arms and changed the concept of Europe from a geographical area to a common cultural heritage. Heroic deeds soon found their way into the chronicles and then percolated down to the popular level of the minstrels, who glorified a new type of hero: the Christian knight, emissary of the Church Triumphant fighting the Unbeliever on her behalf and under her command. Soon going on a crusade would become a part of the code of chivalry, and social pressures, educational patterns and the demands of public opinion would make participation in a crusade obligatory for any self-respecting noble.

Every society is concerned with perpetuating its ideals and life-style, and the noble society of the Middle Ages was no exception. Living example on the one hand and formal education on the other assured the transmission of ideals and the perpetuation of the noble way of life. Schooling, in the modern sense of the word, was almost non-existent in lay society. Education was effected in a far larger measure by the environment than it is today, but the environment was a select one and specially chosen for its task. At a very young age, when the child was just old enough to dispense with his mother's constant attention, he would be sent to another lordly household. Here he was taught the elements of religion by a cleric and was also introduced to the type of seigniorial life he would lead in the future. Though a lordly household had a large number of domestics, the adolescent was assigned to serve one of the knights, often a member of the lord's family or of his retinue. Thus he became familiar with a noble's daily chores, from the care of horses and hounds to that of the harness, armour and arms. He rode to the hunt – as much pastime as para-military exercise – with his tutor and the seigniorial household. At an early stage he would begin mounted exercises with a sword, lance and shield. At the same time the young page was introduced to feminine society and the finer aspects of social life.

Religious education, though not very profound, was certainly the adolescent's major spiritual experience. The teaching of the creeds and biblical narratives, psalmody, the rites of the great feasts of the Christian calendar, and traditions of the local saints, monasteries and churches was for many the greatest influence upon their future course in life. Reading and writing were not universal even among the nobility, though some nobles were destined for the Church and consequently received an academic education from childhood. In any case, few great lords ever wrote either personal or official letters, as a hired cleric would normally fulfil this task. Reading was more common, and reading meant a knowledge of Latin, in which the greater part of Europe's cultural legacy was preserved. Moreover, as Latin was the language of the Church, at least rudimentary knowledge of the language was a necessity, though a noble would undoubtedly know the most common prayers and hymns by heart.

At the time of the First Crusade, or perhaps a generation or two earlier, literature began to be written in the vernacular – first in German and then in French, Spanish and Italian, where it faced stronger competition with Latin. Created for the new type of society, the vernacular literature reflected the enlargement of its audience and new habits and forms of social life. This, in turn, introduced new demands on the education of the scion of a noble house. Frequenting gatherings attended by ladies, the young squire had to learn the customs and the mores of the court, the ' *courtoisie* '. This consisted not only of special behaviour, but included skills and knowledge required by the new patterns of socialising. The squire was expected to be able to compose poems, or at least rhyme for the occasion, and sing to his own accompaniment. These intellectual accomplishments, together with the demands of grace and courtesy, formed a counterpart to his martial education, which ultimately was the most important for his future.

According to a common saying, riding began when the child could walk. This was as much a necessity as a symbol of status. A man's military performance and skill depended on his mastery of the horse. Riding for pleasure and together with the hunt introduced the young-ster to the use of arms. Mastering the bow and arrow, less important in military exercises, proved its value when hunting with hounds or falcons. Then followed the wielding and throwing of the javeline or lance, using a shield and handling a mace, sword or dagger. Elements of strategy and tactics were learned through living example when the squire accompanied a knight on one of the innumerable *chevauchées* which destroyed the crops of a neighbouring landlord. Watch on the castle battlements and the art of siege, though seldom the art of con-structing siege machines, rounded out his military education.

Thus a young man grew up in a double framework of life: fighting and courtly life. The romances of chivalry, as well as the medieval lyrics and courtly poetry, represented these two aspects of his educa-tion, the dual aims of life, two different levels of existence, the ideals of heroism and the ideals of a courtly, refined society. One pro-claimed the great virtues of his half-barbarian ancestors, the other those of a society which, contemporary with the literary outburst, would soon create the marvels of the Romanesque and Gothic in architecture, sculpture and painting.

Courtly behaviour was seldom touched by religion, and the Church took more than a sceptical view of some of its ideals, like those which to all purposes divorced marriage from love. The latter, which spurred men on to marvellous deeds, was presumed to exist between the lord's unattainable wife and the young squire. Whether this situa-tion, so often described in the poetry of the time, was a literary creation devised to add an element of drama or tragedy, or whether it reflected a common practice of adultery is anybody's guess. It is quite possible that the nostalgia and yearnings of high-born ladies and young nobles did not climax in sighing and *courtoisie* but created a double framework of intimate cohesion: marriage by convention and the rearing of a family for the perpetuation of the true blue-blooded lignage; and love (i.e., romantic love) flourishing outside the marital framework. Certainly the Church did not tolerate this mode of existence; but beyond preaching chastity and threatening anathema it could hardly intervene. Still, one should always keep in mind the fact that this type of mentality and behaviour was restricted to a very limited circle of society.

On the other hand, as mentioned earlier, the Church took the lead in transforming the fighting man into a Christian knight. Once the profession of arms became acceptable, the Church intervened in the major event of the noble's life: the rite of knighting. Nothing was nearer to the heart of medieval man than rites and symbols. This mentality was partially a legacy of earlier belief in the magic of the rite and the spoken word and partially the outcome of living in a world directed by Providence and yet inhabited or influenced by the Devil and his acolytes, a world that everyday language described only with difficulty, a reality more easily expressed by the symbol, which was often taken for reality itself. In this perspective, knighting became as much a proclamation that the youngster had become man as a rite studded with symbols and symbolic gestures, a kind of a condensed catechism of virtues to be followed by the knighted youngster.

Though the ceremony of knighting was based upon and drew its inspiration from the tribal customs of puberty rites, the original elements of the ceremony were now submerged in additions which transformed the social and military act into a Christian rite of baptism – a second baptism, as it were, by which the adult consciously assumes the obligations of taking the sacrament. Like any religious rite, knighting had its contemplative and ritual aspects. In its most elaborated form, it began by the young squire spending a night in a church or chapel. During this 'vigil' he was supposed to contemplate his future life and conduct, the virtues to be pursued and vices to be abandoned and evaded. This nocturnal seclusion in the solitude of the Lord's temple was the counterpart of contrition in the sacrament of penance and simultaneously marked the turning point in his life. The bath taken on the morning of the knighting, like the sacrament of baptism, was as much a symbolic as a ritual purification, marking the squire's entrance into the new society – not the Community of Believers this time, but the Christian brotherhood of aristocratic warriors. Confession and mass opened the day of the great event. The new vestments worn for the occasion, resplendent in their whiteness, proclaimed purity of heart and intent. All these preparations were taken from the Church.

Moreover, the Church intervened at the very core of the rite, since from the end of the eleventh century onward the priest (one may even say the priest officiating at the knighting) blessed the material symbols of knighthood: the sword and the lance or the *gonfanon* (almost all paraphernalia of the warrior, with the exception of spurs) which were handed over during the act of knighting.

The actual act of bestowing knighthood was done by an older man, himself a knight. He might have been the young man's father or relative, but very often he was someone renowned for his chivalrous behaviour. In some instances knighthood was even bestowed by an ecclesiastic. The man who performed the ceremony helped the young squire to gird the sword, then gave him his lance, helmet and spurs. The young man fell to his knees and received the accolade, or stroke on the shoulder, a symbolic act whose meaning is not entirely clear. According to one theory, it was meant to remind him of the memorable event all his life; according to others, it was proof that the man could stand the blow. One way or another, it was an axiomatic assumption that this was the only time in life that a knight may endure a blow without taking offence and without returning it.

Naturally, the elaborateness of the knighting ceremony depended on the standing of the family. In princely households it became a major festivity; for lesser families it was modest. Despite the natural propensity to institutionalise the ceremony of knighting, an earlier, and in a sense more original, tradition of knighting or dubbing the young man on the battlefield when he proved his valour did not disappear. This remained a path, albeit narrow, of mobility and allowed even a commoner to enter the nobility.

By the beginning of the twelfth century, the defence and protection of the faith were counted among the new duties of a knight. Medieval man looked upon Emperor Heraclius and upon Charlemagne as the illustrious examples of Defenders of the Faith. Very soon, a new example rose in the popular imagination, that of the Maccabees, the great heroes of sacred history who bodily defended their faith against the sacrilegious heathens. One could fight the pagan Prussians on the frontiers of Germany and Poland or the Moslem infidel in Spain, but there was nothing more glorious than marching off to war in the Holy Land. To fight for the faith, to liberate or defend the Holy Sepulchre of the Lord became part and parcel of the code of chivalry. It was as much a religious as a knightly obligation. Taking leave of his beloved at the time of the Third Crusade, Canon de Béthune declared:

Alas, sweet Love, what heart-breaking separation from that most wonderful who was ever loved and served . . . Sighing and in love to Syria I must go, as nobody should fail his Creator . . . To great and humble let it be known that it is there that one performs chivalry. It is there that one gains Paradise and honour, prize and praise and the love of the beloved.

Paradise and honour, praise and love – the prizes of life on earth and of eternal bliss. Religious teachings and the elements of chivalry fused together; the earthly and the heavenly were inseparably linked in a harmonious code of life. Again and again the combined ideals are evoked in contemporary poetry, stressing that Christendom's honour was at stake. The domination of Jerusalem by its mortal foes made Christian life shameful. The knights who join the crusade fulfil their duties not only for themselves but for Christendom at large. To quote Canon de Béthune again: 'Clerics and old men who will perform good deeds and charity – all will have a share in the pilgrimage; so also the ladies, if only they live in chastity and preserve loyalty to those who parted there.' He adds, as a kind of afterthought, a few lines which must have been on the mind of more than one crusader: 'But if the ladies, badly inspired, will sin – alas, they will sin with cowards and the bad only, as all the good men will be on the pilgrimage.' This very human reflection would be voiced again a hundred years later by the French troubadour Rutebeuf, who rebuffed all those who opposed the Crusades, including those for whom parting from a loved one was a major obstacle to their participation.

From taking the cross and the oath of the crusade until the departure, time was needed to finance the expedition, find companions and possibly choose a leader for the voyage. These tasks were easy when the great crusades were proclaimed by the papacy and were headed by kings or princes. But in between these great expeditions, countless knights and commoners made their way to the Holy Land, enjoying the special status of 'crusaders' bestowed upon them by the Church. These privileges included not only the remission of sins and protection of lives and possessions, but even freezing debts and interest until their return. 'Going on a crusade', like everything else in the code of chivalry, turned into a rite. It began with taking an oath of obligation to depart for the Holy Land, administered by a priest before the assembled population of castle and manor. The potential crusader would sew red crosses on his coat or tunic, often on the shoulders, back and breast. This was a sign that the crusader was bent on fighting for no other reason but the glory of the faith and the cross. But often a whole year or more passed until the knight was really ready for the expedition.

The departure was celebrated by a ceremony in the chapel of the castle or at a nearby church or monastery. After confession and communion, the crusader took his arms, sword, lance, shield and pennon, which had been consecrated and blessed at the altar. From here he proceeded in the company of family, neighbours and peasants to the gates of the castle or the boundary of his manor. Parting was difficult. Medieval men, though often on the road, were seldom absent from their homes for long periods, unless they were professional merchants (and even then, several months away from home would be regarded as an extraordinary adventure). Going to the Holy Land usually meant two years of absence, and these often turned into even longer periods. This was so, of course, if the man was lucky enough to return at all, for thousands and tens of thousands never came back. Some died on the road of disease or exhaustion; others were captured at sea by Moslem (and sometimes Christian) pirates; not to mention those who died on the battlefields of Armenia, Syria, Egypt and the Holy Land or were captured and cast into Moslem captivity, waiting long years for an occasion to let their nearest king know and ask for ransom money. Joinville, the famous biographer of St Louis, thus describes his own departure for the crusade:

On Friday I said to them: 'My friends, I'm soon going overseas, and I do not know whether I shall ever return. So will any of you who have a claim to make against me come forward. If I have done you any wrong, I will make it good.' And in order not to influence their decision I withdrew from the discussion, and afterwards agreed without demur to whatever they recommended. Since I did not wish to take away with me a single penny to which I had no right, I mortgaged the greater part of my land. I can assure you that on the day I left our country to go to the Holy Land I had in my possession an income of no more than a thousand livres from my estates. On the day I left Joinville I sent for the abbot of Cheminon, who was said to be the wisest and worthiest monk of the Cistercian Order. This same abbot of Cheminon gave me my pilgrim's staff and scrip. I left Joinville immediately after – never to enter my castle again until my return from overseas – on foot, with my legs bare and dressed in my shirt. Thus attired I went to Blécourt and Saint-Urbain, and to other places where there are holy relics. And all the way to Blécourt and Saint-Urbain I never once let my eyes turn back towards Joinville, for fear my heart might be filled with longing at the thought of my lovely castle and the two children I had left behind.

It was thus with a heavy heart that one took leave of his home, family and homeland. A charming and touching poem by an otherwise unknown lady poet, whose name might have been Jehan (Jeanne) de Neuville, contains the following lines:

> Jerusalem, you made me suffer greatly,
> Taking away what I loved most.
> Note I'll never love thee,
> Because there is nothing which filled me with more joy.
> Often I'm so oppressed and so angry
> That I hold it against God,
> Who took my greatest joy away from me.
> Sweet *bel ami* how can you allow
> My great suffering, there over the salty sea?
> Nothing can describe the pain which my heart endures
> When I remember your sweet clear face,
> Which I used to kiss and caress,
> It is a marvel that I don't lose my senses.

It is feelings such as these in the context of the Crusades which explain a unique piece of twelfth-century sculpture, preserved at the Cordeliers in Nancy. It probably represents an historical personage, the count of Vendôme, who joined the host of his king, Louis VII, on the Second Crusade but was not among those who returned one year later (1148). Mourned, declared lost and all but forgotten, he returned to his native land fifteen years later. The sculpture represents the reunion of the returning count – still in tatters, wearing cross and supported by a pilgrim's staff – and his wife. The embracing bodies seem to have fused into one block of stone – a silent stone but one more expressive than any episode in a chivalric romance.

The strength of the tie between chivalry and the Crusades can best be gauged by the fact that it remained in force for two hundred years.

opposite The citadel of Jerusalem, goal of the Crusades, with the Temple esplanade in the background

Counted in medieval terms, that is some ten successive generations of almost uninterrupted movement to the Orient. And would remain alive for another two hundred years, culminating in military expeditions against the Mameluks, Mongols and Turks, though its heyday was over.

There is something extremely captivating about these medieval nobles bent on chivalrous adventure. They were undoubtedly moved by an intense faith, although one may be sceptical about the depth of their religiosity. Faith was part of their upbringing and everyday life; a never-questioned reality which accompanied feasts and seasons and all major events in a man's life from birth to burial. The Crusades were born of faith, and faith was rekindled by the Crusades. Fighting the Infidel and liberating or defending the Holy Sepulchre was not only a slogan, an outlet for war and fighting, but an aspect of one's inner life and sense of obligation.

Nonetheless, these mighty warriors nurtured on the Bible and romances of chivalry were also the audience of the troubadour's frivolous outlook on life, which frankly preached permissiveness and adultery. There was no objective bridge between the two but the reality of a life in which one practised both without trying to harmonise them. In all probability, many followed the path indicated in some moralising writings of the period – that is, regretting in age the frivolities and excesses of youth. Yet the double practice of chivalry and *courtoisie* was not the only form of behaviour. If *courtoisie* contributed the enchantments of love and enticements of sexual pleasures to the severe duties of a Christian warrior for the great majority, others found it despicable. Not only the clergy, but solid segments of the the laity found the double standard of morals repugnant.

If Provence, with its exaltation of love, captured the north, the Holy Land reacted and captured all of the West by creating another ideology of the perfect Christian knight. His dreams were filled not with images of profane love but with visions of sacred love, the love of the Eternal. Moral teachings and Christian virtues inculcated in childhood claimed their own and were strengthened and invigorated by contact with the Holy Land, which became the cradle of the military orders. The most original creation of the crusaders and of the Crusades, the orders were the most sublime realisation of the two great ideologies of medieval Europe—monastic life and knighthood—and became one of the most profound expressions of the ethos of the Middle Ages.

The idea behind the military orders did not generate among clerics or monks. Its initiators were laymen, and the orders were one of the earliest creative efforts of the noble class in the realm of ethics and ideology. Immediately after the crusaders captured Jerusalem, a Provençal knight named Gerald gathered a group of knights to care for the sick and wounded. The stench of cadavers strewn in the streets still filled the city when the small company of knights began its charitable work in an improvised hospital. The concept of a hospice and hospital were not new. About 1070 a group of merchants from Amalfi who frequented the Levant had established a hospice for Western pilgrims in Jerusalem. Hospice and hospital ceased to function during the siege, and the monks and nuns who cared for the sick were probably expelled from the city. The innovation of the new institution was in the fact that it was laymen – knights – not monks and nuns, who assumed the care of the sick, humble and needy. Charity, as commonly viewed by the nobility, meant giving alms to the needy and the gesture was generally accompanied by condescension. Following the late-classical imagery of the struggle between the virtues and vices, medieval representations of *caritas* depicted king and noble visiting the sick, but certainly never taking care of them personally. The small group of knights who gathered around Gerald in Jerusalem thus made a unique contribution in the sphere of social consciousness.

The knights established themselves just across from the southern entrance to the area of the Holy Sepulchre. They took over a curious, two-storey Byzantine church whose main feature was a tri-lobed lower chapel. The patron saint of the church, St John the Almsgiver of Alexandria, was soon replaced by a more popular figure, St John the Baptist. The former Amalfi hospice and nunnery of St Mary were integrated in the complex of hospital buildings, which soon expanded and took up a whole city quarter. In a war-ridden state which was nonetheless visited by thousands each year, care of the sick and wounded was an urgent necessity. Soon donations and gifts from pilgrims and royal and noble houses overseas arrived to strengthen the financial position of the community.

This voluntary association of idealists adopted the rules of a monastic association, and its members took the triple vows of poverty, chastity and obedience. For almost a generation it seemed that the order's future would be that of a monastic institution with hospitaller aims. Once inside a monastic institution, a noble did not differ – at least in theory –

from any other monk, though his birth and education might have been a factor in promoting him to a place of honour, like that of prior or abbot. But in a country characterised by a large influx of immigration, which was true of the Latin kingdom, it would have been difficult to keep to the rules which discriminated noble and non-noble. Ultimately, if the Order of St John did not follow this path of evolution and continued to discriminate between the two, it was because a new type of noble association had come into being in the meantime, the Order of the Templars.

The Order of the Templars—so called because its earliest abode was in the 'Temple of Solomon' in Jerusalem (that is, in the Mosque of al-Aqsa) – was built upon different premises which, in a sense, were far more congenial to the social class whose members joined its ranks. It was established by Hugh de Payns, who gathered a small group of knights in a voluntary association to serve as armed convoys for pilgrims on their way from Jerusalem to Jericho and thence to the traditional place of Jesus's baptism in the Jordan. The general state of insecurity during the first two decades of the kingdom's existence was not only due to poorly defended borders and insufficient fortifications. It was felt quite keenly within the borders of the kingdom as well, since the population of the countryside remained Moslem, and Crusader authority extended only as far as the power to dominate the native population by force. The Moslems remained hostile. Some even abandoned their homesteads and migrated to Syria and Egypt; others, we learn from a Crusader chronicle, left their land fallow, preferring to live on the verge of starvation and thus deprive the hated conquerors of means of income. Travel was extremely dangerous in the hilly and mountainous regions of Judea and Galilee, making a pilgrimage to St John's Ford, Bethlehem or Nazareth a hazardous venture. The situation was no better on the main road from the port of Jaffa through the plain of Ramle to Jerusalem. To protect the pilgrims, the Templars organised military convoys which became part of Crusader scenery.

This early military association soon evolved into a community of the pledged. Some rudimentary rules may already have been laid down already by the founder in 1118 and were officially incorporated into the rules of the order when it received ecclesiastical sanction. The new association received moral backing from the outstanding spiritual authority of the period, St Bernard of Clairvaux. In a small pamphlet called *On the Praise of the New Knighthood*, Bernard left us a description of the ideal type of a Templar, in contrast to the worldly knight. Of the worldly knight, bent on soft living and personal glory, he wrote:

You bedeck your horses with silk, you overlay your armour with flowing overcoats. Your lances are painted; so are your shields and your saddles. You stud your bridles and stirrups with gold, silver and precious stones. And with all that pomp, moved by a shameful fury and impudent stupidity, you go to battle. Are these the emblems appropriate to a knight, or are they rather ornaments suitable for a woman? Do you really think that the enemy's sword respects gold, saves precious stones and does not penetrate silken garments? I learned from experience that a fighter needs three things: he should be a brave knight, alert, careful to protect himself; he should be swift; and he should be always ready to strike. But you, on the contrary, you let your hair grow long like women, so that it obstructs your sight; you hamper your movements because of the long, floating tunics; you bury your delicate and tender hands in over-ample sleeves, which float around you.

And here is the 'knight of God', the Templar, as contemplated by the spiritual leader of Europe:

First of all, there is discipline and unqualified obedience. Everybody comes and goes according to the will of the commander. Everybody wears the dresses given to him, and no one goes about searching for food or garments according to his whims. In food and vestments, one is content with the most necessary, avoiding anything superfluous. They live in a community, soberly and in joy, without wife and children. And to reach evangelical perfection, they live in the same house, in the same manner, without calling anything their own, solicitous to preserve the unity of spirit in the bonds of peace.

Impudent words, senseless occupations, immoderate laughter, whispering or even suppressed giggling are unknown. They have a horror of chess and dice; they hate hunting; they don't even enjoy the flight of the falcon. They despise mimes, jugglers, story-tellers, dirty songs, performances of buffoons – all these they regard as vanities and inane follies. They cut their hair short because they know that it is shameful for a man to wear it long. Never overdressed, they bathe rarely and are dirty and hirsute, tanned by the coat of mail and the sun.

The new order met with tremendous success. It was favoured by the local king and nobles because it fulfilled one of the kingdom's urgent needs; but its appeal was immediately felt throughout Christendom, and branches of the order were established in almost every country. The vow of poverty of the founding knights remained in force for the individual, but not for the collectivity. The white mantles and new crosses of the Templars soon symbolised power and wealth. The order's success could have been expected, as it fused the two great ideologies of the period – monasticism and chivalry. A member was able to exercise his most natural inclinations – the product of his social environment and education – under the aegis of the Church with the full knowledge that his military occupation was for the greater glory of God. Here was a fusion of chivalry and *courtoisie* for those who took a more sober view of the meaning of Christian life and the duties of a Christian noble. Noble and knight eagerly joined the new order in Europe, hoping one day to be transferred to its headquarters and major scene of activity in the Christian colonies of the East. Those who did not feel strongly enough to join the order for life soon found a way to affiliate themselves temporarily by serving for several years. The emblem which was allegedly painted on the Templars' banner, the *Beauseant*, carried a verse from the Psalms: 'Not unto us, O Lord, not unto us, but unto Thy name give glory.'

A legend soon sprang up about the miraculous antiquity of the order. It was not Hugh de Payns, the Provencal knight, who founded it; its origins were pushed back twelve hundred years to the restorers and defenders of the Temple: the Maccabees! These Jewish national heroes who liberated their country from the Hellenistic rulers of Syria in the second century before Christ, the purifiers of Jerusalem and restorers of the Temple, became the ancestors of the Templars.

The emergence and the sensational success of the Templars had immediate repercussions within the older Order of St John. Founded a generation earlier, it now had to compete with the strong appeal exercised by the Templars. The Hospitallers faced the challenge by adding military duties to their obligations, and soon black mantles and eight pointed crosses would identify the military contingents of the order. They would become not just an integral part of the kingdom's army, but – together with contingents of other military orders – its very standing army. Whereas the feudal host had to be mobilised anew for every emergency, the military orders were an army of knights permanently on alert, always ready for action.

From the mid-1130s the two military orders not only supplied contingents to the kingdom's army but assumed the defence of key military positions. Fortified points, towers and castles were handed over to the orders, and soon the whole network of roads and communications, was policed by their patrols. Moreover, from the second half of the twelfth century, with the growth of the Moslem threat, the orders implanted themselves in the huge castles which defended the borders of the kingdom and the northern Crusader establishments. In the principality of Antioch and the county of Tripoli, almost the entire border which faced the Moslem states was guarded by contingents of the military orders. In the circumstances peculiar to the northern establishments, the orders all but created independent states with their own foreign policy. The Crusader princes even had to acknowledge that their treaties with the neighbouring Moslem states would not be valid unless accepted by the military orders.

In the face of the military orders' spectacular rise in importance, power and wealth, one wonders what happened to the lofty ideals of selfless service and poverty so strongly and unequivocally stressed by titles like the 'Poor Fellow-Knights of Christ' or the 'Servants of the Poor of Christ'. The orders grew rich through grant and privilege. The Hospitallers allegedly possessed 18,000 manors in Europe. The Templars, hardly poorer, ironically became the great European bankers of the thirteenth century, vying with the banking houses of Italy and even with the Lombards and Cahorsins, the most notorious usurers of medieval Europe. On the one hand, the safety of their well-guarded castles and towers, called 'the Temples' for short, assured the security of the deposits, and their standing as members of the Church turned the orders' property into asylums against lay intervention. On the other, the orders' many branches facilitated the transfer of obligations and credits from place to place without actually transporting money over dangerous roads and seas. Deposits and transfers were remunerated, and the accumulated liquid capital was used to provide loans to king and princes. No wonder, then, that Europe simultaneously praised and blamed the orders. Praises were heaped upon their valour, military skill and devotion to Christendom. But these were counterbalanced by trenchant criticism of their wealth, censure of their alleged greed and condemnation of the rivalries which undermined the stability, and even the very existence, of the Crusader kingdom.

Neither the Hospitallers nor Templars created independent states in the original Crusader establishments, but the Templars almost became rulers of Cyprus in the thirteenth century, and the Hospitallers ruled Rhodes and then Malta until Napoleon conquered it. But another, similar institution which was slowly growing into a full-fledged order at the turn of the twelfth century followed a different destiny. Syria, Lebanon and the Holy Land – lands of Crusader immigration and colonisation – faced the problem of integrating the newcomers. Social and cultural dominance of the French element was almost universal. Though Latin was used in correspondence, French was, from the beginning, the spoken language of the population. The Italians spoke their own dialects among themselves but used French in external contacts. Whereas the French of central and northern France was spoken in the Latin kingdom, Antioch used Norman French and Tripoli Occitan or Provençal. But situations arose in which the use of the 'lingua franca' was insufficient. The sick and pilgrims, especially commoners, would naturally seek someone who spoke their native language. It was in such circumstances that in the twelfth century a hospice and a hospital dedicated to St Mary, part of the Order of St John, became a rallying point for German-speaking pilgrims.

The German hospice, though part of the Order of St John, enjoyed some kind of autonomy, as it had its own prior. Its activities ceased with the capture of Jerusalem by Saladin in 1187. The fall of the capital aroused Europe to a new military expedition, the Third Crusade. It was during the almost three-year siege of Acre, with its thousands wounded in battle or decimated by climate and food, that the need for a special hospital to care for the German-speaking crusaders became stringent. Merchants and sailors from the Baltic Sea, Bremen and Hamburg, established an improvised field hospital, a kind of wooden barrack constructed from the timber of dismantled ships and protected against sun and rain by the canvas of sails. And then, as a hundred years earlier in the Order of St John, a group of German knights and priests dedicated itself to the task of charity. A few years later the improvised establishment became a new military order, the Teutonic Order or the Order of St Mary of the Teutons, which combined charitable services with the military objectives.

Thus three military orders dominated the Crusader scene of the thirteenth century, but whereas the Hospitallers and Templars kept to their international character, the Teutonic Order became the iron fist of German expansion. Like the older orders, the Teutonic knights valiantly participated in all the wars and military expeditions in the Holy Land. They acquired land and castles, like Montfort in Galilee, but their hearts were elsewhere. Their direct links with Germany oriented them to the marches of eastern Germany rather than the marches of oriental Christendom. They tried in vain to establish a foothold in Hungary, but at the invitation of the Polish count of Masovia (1231), they successfully implanted themselves in the Baltic belt of Prussia and thus laid the foundations of the future Kingdom of Prussia and the cornerstone of Imperial Germany.

The notion of the warrior-monk soon acquired a series of imitators. One military order in particular, though it never reached the status of the great ones, is curious and typical enough of the Crusader milieu to merit attention. This was the Order of St Lazarus, created in Jerusalem in the middle of the twelfth century. Its name points to its peculiarity, for this was the Order of Leper knights. The monstrous sickness of leprosy a malady without a remedy, seems to have been rampant in the Near East. As it was regarded as being highly contagious, its victims were shut away from the world outside the city walls and castle gates. The crusaders found another solution. A hospital and enclosure outside but leaning on the walls of Jerusalem became a lepers' colony, but its knights and commoners associated themselves into a military order. One can imagine them attacking the Moslems and sowing panic as much by their military valour as by their threat of contagion.

In passing, mention should also be made of smaller orders which sprang up in the Crusader kingdom – such as military orders of Italian knights or the English Order of St Thomas of Canterbury – although none of them ever played a major role in the kingdom. More important was the fact that the idea which originated in the Holy Land was seized upon by Europe, and in addition to the great international orders, local military orders came into being, especially in the lands which faced a Moslem or pagan antagonist. Thus Spain and Portugal, and later on Lithuania and Poland, had their own military orders modelled on the Palestinian example. Some of them played a role in the history of the Iberian Peninsula; others in that of the eastern Baltic. It was the centripetal force of monarchy which brought about their incorporation into the existing structure of state and society in almost every case. Their disappearance at the end of the Middle Ages or beginning of the Reformation did not stir much protest in public opinion. By then the ideals of monasticism and chivalry were partially discredited. And in the sixteenth century, Cervantes would reduce the glorious knight to the figure of Don Quixote, a misguided anachronism who ventured into the age of the Renaissance.

...sante Babilonis cogit. et xpus ex alto
.pspicie sppuram bumana ofundir lm
gua. ne se muicem dedificantes intelligãt.
Atqi ita ceptum opus non possit impleri.

Western masons and stone-cutters at work. In the art of siege and
fortifications, the crusaders learned from the Orient. Detail from a 13th-
century illuminated Latin manuscript depicting the construction of the Tower
of Babel (74)

left Caesarea Maritima of Herodian fame became the Crusader Cesaire. The walls, jetty and ruins of the castle are on the left; sixty Herodian columns laid in the shallow water (extreme right) served as a makeshift northern jetty (75)

right St Louis dotted the kingdom with a stone ring of fortifications. The fortified main entrance to Caesarea (76)

left A promontory transformed into a fortress. Ruins of the Pilgrim's Castle of the Templars, with the city walls and church in the foreground (77)

right Crusader fortifications were influenced by the East, but oriental influence stopped at the threshold of the churches. A romanesque bas-relief of St Matthew from the Hospitallers' castle of Belvoir in Galilee (78)

above Bearded Moslem
warriors defend their city
as Crusader knights use
stone-throwing catapults,
while St George (on right)
encourages the assault. An
oriental Christian from the
city (possibly Antioch)
guides the knights scaling
the ladder (79)

left Fighting men and
demons. Crusaders assault
a city with siege towers
while Moslem warriors
man the defences and
witches recite incantations
(80)

right A pottery receptacle for
'Greek fire', the deadly napalm of
the medieval Orient (81)

below The first rule of warfare:
demoralise the enemy. The heads
of slaughtered opponents are
paraded on lances before a
besieged city (82)

above No Moslem army could withstand the direct assault of the mailed Crusader knights; the whirlwind swept away everything in its path. Crusader knights clash with the dark-skinned, turban-clad Moslem warriors in this detail from the *History of Godfrey of Bouillon*, 14th century (83)

opposite Expensive chain-mail, used by Moslems (shown here) and crusaders alike, was handed down from generation to generation (84)

left The technique of fighting *à la turque* spread to the Near East from Central Asia. A mounted noble of Mongolian origin in a detail from a 14th-century brass vessel inlaid with silver (85)

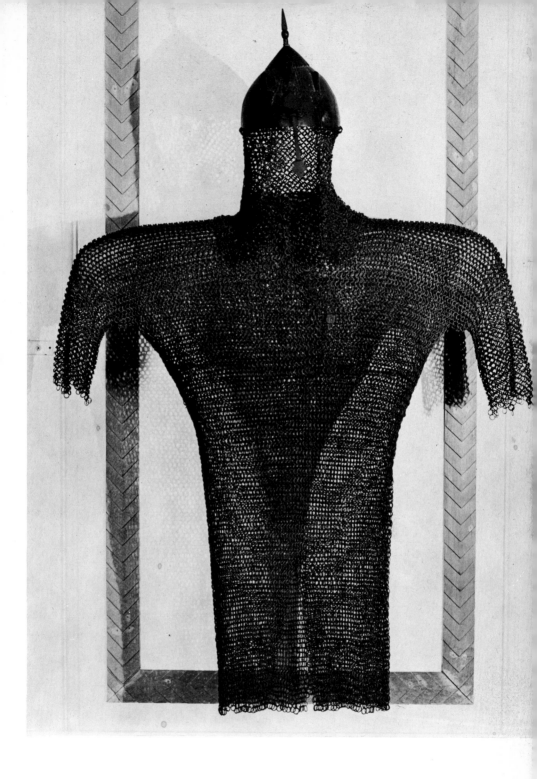

أَنَّسهُ كَلِّ مَنْ غَابَ صَدْرَهُ أُوْلَيْلَ أَهْلَ بَلَدَهُ

المَقامة التاسعة عشرة

رَوَى الحَرَثُ بْنُ هَمَّامٍ قَالَ أَهْلُ العِرَاقِ ذَاكَ العُرْبُ

إخَالَ أَنْوَاءُ العَيْمِ وَنَخَدَّثُ الرُّكْبَانِ بِنَفْنَصِيب

وَبِلَغَنِيَ أَهْلُها المَحِيبَينَ أَتَخِذَ مَهْرَتًا وَأَعْتَقِبْتَ سَهَرَهُم

A Moslem warrior on camel back in the immense sand seas of the Orient (86)

8

Castles and Warfare

A minority destined to rule an enemy majority had no other means to assure its existence than to concentrate in a relatively small number of fortified places, whether cities or castles. Still, these means were hardly sufficient to control the countryside, assure communications and make Frankish presence in the Holy Land a tangible reality. Thus in addition to the fortified city and huge castle, the crusaders dotted the country's network of main and secondary roads with forts and observation points, more like police stations than military bases. The fortifications and garrisons easily communicated from mountain to plain by fire signals or carrier pigeons, a technique which the Franks learned in the East. It was within their means to transfer news quickly and effectively from Transjordan, via Jerusalem, to Jaffa and Acre. The fortified Crusader sites represented the static military establishment; the army was its mobile element.

Fort, castle or city in the Latin kingdom were rarely entirely new. Cities, in particular, were not built by the crusaders but were captured from their former Moslem rulers, and the crusader contribution was normally the elaboration of the existing system of defence. The crusaders often built forts and castles, but even they were usually erected in places which at one time or other in the three millennia of the country's history had been fortified and then abandoned. In such cases the crusaders probably followed the older layout of fortifications, as they surely made use of the foundations of the earlier sites. A local Crusader saying had it that: 'a castle destroyed is already half rebuilt'. The Crusader fortifications ranged from small towers located on the roads to giant castles such as Saphet in Galilee, where the Templars' garrison and administrative staff reached almost 2,000 inhabitants. Such a population would have ranked the place as a city in contemporary Europe. The size of the fortification depended on its site, the available money and manpower and its function. A police station which guarded a road, an administrative centre for the vast domains of a military order or a castle on the marches, which faced a permanent Moslem threat across limitless dunes and desert, had to be constructed differently to fulfil their varied tasks.

Basically, all fortifications had three main units of defence: outer defences, the encircling wall and towers and the central keep or *donjon*. The outer defences were normally composed of a ditch with an escarp and counterescarp and sometimes an outlying tower or observation point. These were followed by a curtain of walls pierced by salient, normally square but sometimes round, towers. The most elaborate array of defences was concentrated near the main gate of the castle. Crusader ditches were almost never flooded, as the 'land of milk and honey' never had enough water to spare. Their main task was to prevent the formidable ram or siege towers from approaching the walls. The ditches were meticulously built, some 45 feet wide and 24–36 feet deep. From the bottom of the ditch rose the outer walls of the fortification. Their base was an inclined, rivetted glacis which was heavy enough to discourage attempts at tunnelling. The glacis normally formed the escarp of the ditch. On this pyramid-like, strong base rose the walls proper, some 50 feet high (or 80 feet from the bottom of the ditch) with crenellated battlements. The towers rose from the curtain of walls and were spaced so that arrows or other missiles launched from them could cover the whole area surrounding the castle. If a second wall existed, it was often twice as high as the outer one and was equipped with high towers which – like the squares of a checkerboard – filled the gaps between the towers of the first wall.

A separate unit in the middle of the castle or at its weakest point, or, alternatively, one of the towers of the second wall, was usually the seat of the ruler or commander. This was the keep or *donjon*. The beautifully preserved keep at Belvoir in Galilee is a two-storey rectangle which included a spacious inner bailey. Built of huge stones of excellent draft, this was the innermost nucleus of the castle. The chapter or seigniorial hall led on to the inner courtyard, which was surrounded by the lodgings of the knights, the kitchen, the well and other paraphernalia of everyday life. A second storey, reached by an exterior staircase, was taken up by the chapel, offices, commanders' room and additional lodgings. The corners of the keep were reinforced by high towers which were mounted by an inside staircase.

The defences of the gates were usually between two towers, higher than the wall curtain. In Caesarea they were three stories high with a spacious battlement for the defenders and their artillery. Walls and towers were pierced by loopholes, and it was calculated that in Chastel Pèlerin eighty archers could shoot their arrows simultaneously from the many-tiered loopholes. The gate was a defence complex in itself. A bridge which spanned the ditch before the castle lead to the gate. The entire bridge or part thereof was constructed of timber supported on arches or by a column in the middle of the ditch. This enabled the defenders to burn the bridge in case of attack and thus cut off the city from the surrounding area. The gate itself had two huge wooden wings which revolved on pivots, and it was locked from within by a strong beam which entered sockets in the walls. Behind the wooden, metal-studded gate was an iron portcullis operated from the upper storey by a windlass. The gates, always 'L'-shaped to prevent direct penetration in case of a successful attack, were defended on the inside by an open, second-storey gallery from which archers could shoot at the invading enemy.

The clash of West and East in the Holy Land, which took place on every level, placed the crusaders before challenges for which their original military experience had not prepared them. Though the art of siege was known in the early Middle Ages, the Orient presented problems seldom encountered in Europe. The size of the castles, and even more so of the cities with their miles of perimeter walls, made siege, sealing them off and starving out their inhabitants (the normal procedure in the West) inappropriate in the Levant. Maritime cities created an even graver problem, as the crusaders, typical 'landlubbers', lacked fleets and maritime experience. In these circumstances, the art of siege developed around storm and penetration, rather than regular processes of siege and blockade. True, one could spear the heads of captives on lances and parade them below the city ramparts, as was the custom in both East and West; but although this could break the spirit of the besieged, it did not destroy the walls. As the provisions of cities and castles could last not only for months, even years, and there was little chance of starving them into capitulation, they had to be taken by storm.

In the formidable array of weaponry used in the siege of cities, the place of honour went to the mobile siege-tower, often called the 'belfry' because of its shape and height. This structure, several stories high and taller than the besieged ramparts, was composed of a series of platforms manned by the attackers, whereas the top floor was equipped with small pieces of artillery and a bridge which could be lowered to the battlements. The difficulties in using such towers, besides their enormous cost, were manifold. No manor carpenter was able to build a tower some 45–60 feet high, able to carry several dozen warriors; experienced engineers were needed to construct it. It is quite possible that at the early stage of the conquest the crusaders profited from the know-how of the local Christians (the Armenians are mentioned in this connection) in constructing their siege machinery. Another difficulty was bringing the siege-tower, transported on wheels or tree trunks, as close as possible to the walls. This required filling in ditches some 45–60 feet wide and 36 feet deep. Amassing stones, debris and wood to fill in parts of the ditch was a menial job, and it is symptomatic of the crusaders that one of the laws of the kingdom formally stated that a knight was not obliged to dismount even in time of siege! Then there was the permanent danger, time and again attested by the chroniclers, that the besieged would burn the tower in a successful sortie or by using the awe-inspiring 'Greek fire', a chemical compound of sulphur, resin and other inflammable materials invented by the Byzantines. The mixture was placed in earthenware receptacles, ignited and then thrown or catapulted against the tower to deadly effect. Often used in sea battles, where it burned both sail and boat, it proved to be quite efficient in land sieges. Sometimes it was not simple receptacles one may call them hand-grenades but explosive barrels which were hurled by catapults. One must read Joinville on his experience in Egypt to appreciate the impression this medieval napalm made on the Westerners:

The Greek fire looked like a large tun of verjuice, and its burning tail was the length of a long sword. In flight it made a noise like thunder, and it seemed a dragon flying through air. It gave off so great a light that you could see our camp as in broad daylight.

The towers' only protection against fire was damp skins of freshly slaughtered beasts or felt soaked in vinegar, both rather impractical in prolonged sieges.

Where siege-towers were unable to master the fortifications, Moslems and crusaders employed other devices to make a breach in the walls. The oldest of these, and still deadly efficient, was the battering ram, an iron-tipped, mast-like piece of timber hanging on chains and projected against the walls by several men. The besieger could not protect himself with his shield, as its coverage was insufficient and it hampered his activity. The ram was consequently covered by a kind of a building or shed strong enough to resist the stones, arrows and fire-missiles of the beseiged. This faithful instrument of siege shared with the 'belfry' one major disadvantage: it could not be manoeuvred across the large fosse of the fortifications unless the ditch was filled—partially at least.

Another method of siege, known from antiquity, was to use pieces of artillery which would dislocate stones in the walls and open a breach for the attacking army. This method was believed to have been of Persian or Turkish origin, though it was known to the Roman and Byzantine armies and may only have been improved by the Orientals. It often played a decisive role in sieges. The artillery was basically of two types. One was a kind of a gigantic bow operated by cords which discharged bolts, often flaming-white pieces of metal; the other, the catapult or mangonel, discharged stones or other projectiles from a spoon-like contraption. Finally there was the ingenious art of tunnelling, that is using sappers to open a tunnel and undermine the walls of the city. Once a point beneath the walls was reached, the timber props of the tunnel were burnt and the tunnel collapsed, bringing down with it a part of the walls.

Though the siege and capture of castles and cities ultimately determined the fate of the kingdom, because their loss swept the ground from under the crusaders' feet, the battles fought on open ground were the more spectacular events in the military annals of the Latin kingdom. The problems faced by the Crusader armies were extremely complex. Not only had they to deal with a foe almost always superior in numbers, but they faced Moslem armies that followed a technique of fighting which (though known to their Byzantine neighbours) was entirely unknown in the Christian West.

The mainstay of the Crusader host was the heavy cavalry. This fact was the result of a development in the West which owed as much to prevalent military theory as it did to the social *milieu* in which the theory developed. It was based on the segregation of an élite military caste from the rank and file of serfs and commoners. The heavy mailed horseman, normally a knight, was always a member of the aristocratic ruling class. Whether a lord or vassal, his whole life centred around war and fighting. His horse, long ago divorced from agricultural chores, was specially trained to carry the heavy load of the rider and his armour. Additional horses might be used to carry the knight to the battlefield, but he would always ride in to battle on a war-horse or charger. Strong and swift horses were meant to be used in direct encounter between horsemen.

These basic characteristics were not entirely immutable, however. The Crusader knights and armies, in permanent contact with both European hosts and Moslem armies, underwent a process of adaptation and integration which was as marked in the tactic of fighting as it was in the far-reaching changes in armour and weaponry. For almost two hundred years, the West sent the flower of its knighthood to the Latin kingdom, and these reinforcements were a decisive influence in keeping Crusader armament in line with European developments. Symptomatic of the times was the decision of the general chapter of the Hospitallers that the knights destined to come from Europe should bring along their own horse and equipment, costly items on the account books of the order. On the other hand, the crusaders borrowed somewhat from the Moslems, though probably less than one would have expected.

The changes in Moslem arms and armour, if there was any evolution at all, were rather slight, and as far as we know were restricted exclusively to the 'softer' parts of the wardrobe, like undergarments and the cut of the outervestments (at least this was so in the second half of the thirteenth century under the Mameluks). Their military equipment depended on ethnic or local traditions. The conquest of Egypt by Saladin and the importation of his Kurdish troops, as well as Turkish troops, from Syria probably made for more uniformity in the Moslem military establishment. With the rise of the Mameluks to power during St Louis's crusade to Egypt, the armament and armour of the Mongol steppes became dominant. A generation later, when the Mameluk sultan Baybars took over Syria and Mesopotamia and pushed back the Mongols to the Iranian kingdom of the Ilkhans, the Mameluk military costume and armament became uniform in the new empire, and its composition was even fixed by law.

The major items in the defensive armament of both Christian and Moslem were the helmet, body armour and shield. In the Crusader camp, all three underwent marked changes from the time of the First Crusade. Body armour, originally stiff and uncomfortable, became lighter, more flexible and at the same time far more reliable. The erstwhile armour, the so-called *broigne*, that is a coat with metal scales or lamellae sewn or riveted on, was worn over a quilted tunic of cloth or leather and reached below the knight's knees, often to his ankles. Split at its lower part, it permitted riding and partially covered the feet, although sometimes the knight wore hose of the same composition to cover his legs. This early version of body armour was replaced by the *hauberk*, that is a coat of mail proper, far more expensive than the *broigne*. The metal lamellae were replaced by interlaced rings or chains of the mail and became independent of undergarment. The *hauberk* often had a collar and long sleeves which ended in mittens.

The corresponding Moslem body armour was far lighter and more flexible. As early as during the First Crusade, the Moslems wore a coat of mail called *zardiya* which was complemented by stockings and leggings, though the *zardiya*, like the corresponding European armour, often reached to the warrior's ankles. The coat of mail, improved by by the art of riveting, remained in use until the beginning of modern times. As it was extremely expensive, it was handed down in families for generations without any marked changes. Rather different from European armour was the Moslem splint armour and laminae armour, which seems to have been inherited from the Asiatic Mongols and Tartars. Each piece of splint was riveted to the quilted cloth beneath, and the pieces were often overlapping. The laminae armour, often decorated with figures or pious verses, was more for ceremonial than practical use. The splint armour performed the task of protection perfectly, but it must have been no less cumbersome than the early *broigne*, especially for a mounted warrior. Far more comfortable was a short mail tunic known as the *brigandine* in Europe and *kazaghand* (later *qarqal*) in the Orient. This was made of either mail proper, metal scales or small metal nails attached to a padding of felt or another, sometimes coloured, expensive cloth.

The Crusader helmet underwent more far-reaching changes. Its prototype during the First Crusade was a conical iron helmet with leather thongs to cover the neck and very often a nose-piece to protect the face. Whereas body armour became stronger but more supple, the helmet developed in two different directions: on the one hand into a small iron cap with a brim, the *chapeau de fer;* on the other into the great helmet known as *casque de Croisade*. The latter, with its large rounded or flat top, was extremely heavy, covered the ears and neck and all but rested on the shoulders. The nose-piece was replaced by a visor with holes through which to breathe. The iron cap, like the great helmet, was worn over a *coif*, or mail hood, linked to the *hauberk*.

The corresponding Moslem helmet did not change very much during the period of the Crusades. Its basic form was that of an elongated egg, hence its name *baida* (i.e., egg). This helmet was a mark of prestige among the Moslems and was often gilded or inlaid with inscriptions from the Koran. Some had nose-pieces and neck coverings in the form of *camail*, but they did not develop an equivalent of the European face guard. In some cases chain-mail was used to cover the face but this was rather exceptional. Plumes or crests seem to be a later addition.

The Crusader shield underwent the most drastic changes. During the First Crusade, it was a large, solid piece of leather-covered wood or wood with metal bands springing like rays from a central boss. It was kite shaped, rounded at the top, and covered the warrior from neck to foot. The shield was certainly more practical in fighting on foot than in a cavalry charge, when it was suspended from the shoulder by a leather band. It was a cumbersome affair but useful as long as body armour was inadequate. With the perfection of body armour, the long shield became obsolete and was replaced by a rounded or triangular small shield which covered breast and abdomen of the mounted knight. The Moslem shield differed from the outset. When the warriors of the First Crusade still heaved their great shields, Moslem cavalry used a light, rounded shield called *turs*. It was usually convex with a horizontal band on the inside and was easy to handle. These shields so differed from those of the crusaders that they became a feature of the conventional Western representations of Moslem fighters.

The three major articles of body defence – the helmet, armour and shield – were supplemented, in time, by a surcoat. This was normally a sleeveless, white garment worn over the body armour. Sometime around the turn of the twelfth century, the surcoat, shield and often the horse's covering began to bear the knight's distinguishing marks. This was the birth of European and Moslem heraldry, which has survived in one form or another up to our own times. Geometrical designs, flowers, beasts and the like were blazoned on the surcoat, shield and pennons, and the terms 'coat-of-arms' and 'shield-of-arms' derive from the surcoat and shield on which the armorial insignia were painted. Originally used it seems, to facilitate recognition of the fully armoured knight in a *mêlée*, the coat-of-arms developed into the

One of the triple bazaars of Jerusalem reconstructed by Queen Melissande in the middle of the 12th century (87)

Jaffa as seen by a European traveller in 1486. Today, nothing remains o

dieval fortifications (88)

above The autonomous quarters of the Italian communes, like the oriental caravanserais, served as market-places and lodgings. The Khan al-Umdan ('Khan of the Columns') in Acre (89)
below The caravan halted at both caravanserais and simple watering-places in the desert. Moslem merchants and travellers resting on their journey (90)

armorial emblem of the noble family. Heraldry became an *art savant*, and the emblems were a proclamation of origin and ticket of entry into the nobility. Heraldry was not restricted to Europe, however. It appears among the Moslems in the twelfth century and became quite common among the ruling Mameluk aristocracy – often in connection with offices and state charges – in the thirteenth century. By then, blazonry had added colour and designs to the hosts of West and East, and the armorial bearing had become a familiar pattern displayed on the fluttering pennons of the lances, the surcoat and the horse's trappings.

The offensive arms of crusaders and Moslems were almost identical, except for the bow used by the mounted warriors of Islam. Foremost among them was the lance (*rumh* in Arabic), which was used as a thrusting weapon but could also be thrown. The Moslems, and possibly also the crusaders, sometimes used a longer, compound lance. The sword, (*saif* in Arabic) double-edged with a round or flattened pommel, was worn in a leather scabbard which hung from neck and shoulder, but was later attached to the waist. The typical sword was straight, but some of the Moslem weapons were curved. The scimitar, curved and broadening towards a point, later became a typical oriental weapon, but it appeared only after the Crusades. The Moslem wooden scabbard was covered by leather or fine cloth, and the sword itself was often ornamented and bejewelled. Strangely enough, despite the renown of the 'Damascene swords', the Moslem blades of excellence were of Indian or Chinese origin, and the expression 'Damascene' actually applied to the metal incrustation or jewellery worked in Syria and not to the metal (iron, steel or combined iron and steel edges) of the blade.

The mace (*dabbus* in Arabic), made of iron or steel, was used by crusader and Moslem alike. Spherical, fluted and hatched, it was a monstrous piece of weaponry used to smash helmets or shields or break bones. The so-called 'Danish' double-edged axe used by the crusaders was not in use among the Moslems, who preferred the single-edged, semi-circular *tabar*. The bow and cross-bow had their own place in Moslem weaponry. Famous bows were made in Damascus, and St Louis's master of ordinance (*artilleur du roi*), John the Armenian, went there to buy horn and glue for making cross-bows.

The change in Crusader military tactics or rather the adaptation to meet the challenges of the oriental armies, was not the result of the clash with the Egyptian foe – the strongest antagonist in the East – but with the armies of Syria and Mesopotamia. The Egyptians were never regarded as a very martial nation. From the twelfth century until the conquest of Egypt by the Ottoman Turks, every European who visited the kingdom on the Nile was impressed by its pacific character. Long before the Fatimids, the rulers of Egypt recruited their main fighting force among the Bedouin tribes in the eastern provinces and the Sinai peninsula. Some tribes, like the Banu Kinana, were renown for their military skill and bravery, and the Egyptian rulers used them to defend the country's eastern frontiers. Strangely enough, the crusaders, who were familiar with the Bedouin and even succeeded in making some of them into their allies (around Ascalon and Gaza, which bordered on the Sinai desert, and in Transjordan at the entrance of the Arabian peninsula), had a rather low opinion of their martial and moral qualities. The Bedouin were regarded as good guides or reconnaissance troops, but when it came to fighting they were no match for the Western armies. The crusaders believed them to be unreliable cowards who joined the winning side at the last moment in order to be at the kill and share the spoils of an unmerited victory. In addition to their local troops, the rulers of Egypt relied to a great degree on mercenary troops or on military companies composed of young slaves converted to Islam and drilled from youth in military skills. These were the forerunners of the Mameluks, who finally took over the kingdom of Egypt from the weakened hands of Saladin's descendants (1250); they were also the forerunners of the future formidable armies of the Janissars. Such regiments were composed of slaves bought in the interior of Africa and white slaves or Mongols bought in the Black Sea area. The former, called *'abd*, were often of Sudanese origin (the name Sudan derives from the Arabic *sawad* = black); the latter were properly called Mameluks.

The crusaders confronted the Egyptian troops with foot archers and light cavalry. Neither type of soldier was new to the crusaders, though at the end of the eleventh century foot archers were an unimportant quality in Western warfare. The Egyptian light cavalry was more mobile than that of the crusaders, but in hand-to-hand fighting the Egyptians seldom won a battle, unless overwhelming numbers or a a successful ambush or stratagem placed them at a marked advantage. Normally the tough nucleus of the caliph's army or that of his vizier (the Fatimid caliphs seldom left their palaces and harems) was composed of troops of Mameluk origin. These troops were better skilled and were usually loyal to their commander. Often the battle was decided by these élite troops, with their flight or success directly influencing the other regiments of the Egyptian army.

The situation was entirely different vis-à-vis the armies of Mesopotamia, Syria and Persia, which sometimes joined in war against the crusaders. In addition to Arab tribes which roamed Mesopotamia and Syria and the local city militia, the *askars*, the main strength of these armies was the Seljuq Turks. Though more than a hundred years had elapsed since they left their native lands in Central Asia to make their fortunes in the Near East, these former nomads never forgot their traditional technique of fighting, that is *à la turque*. The essential element in this type of warfare was the mounted archer. The style of warfare was ancient and is even described in the Bible: 'A people cometh from the north . . . They shall lay hold on bow and spear; they are cruel and have no mercy; their voice roareth like the sea and they ride upon horses, set in array as men for war against thee' (Jeremiah 6, 22–3). Lightly equipped and charging on swift but sturdy horses, the Turks presented a challenge to the Crusader armies. Not only were they far more mobile than the heavily mailed Western knights, but their concept of war and battle was entirely different.

The strength of the Crusader armies lay in their heavy cavalry, whose charge mowed down everything in its path. The shock of its force, the impact of the iron-clad knights, was irresistible. The result of the battle was often decided during the first encounter, unless the opponent could move forward reinforcements or its flanks could close and attack the assaulting army. But the Turkish opponent was not very cooperative and seldom agreed to a pitched battle and putting up a closed front to be destroyed by the Westerners. Not only was he mobile, but he had brought with him from the Mongolian steppes the deadly bow. The Turks did not enter into direct contact but would discharge a hail of arrows at a gallop from a distance of some eighty metres, where the weapons of the Westerners—lance and javelin, not to mention the sword—could not reach them. The arrows could hardly miss the great, solid mass of mounted knights. In a static position, the crusaders were simply sitting ducks. An attempt to attack a Moslem army was like chasing the wind; it simply disappeared beyond the horizon. The situation was no better when the Crusader host was on the move. Time and again, the Moslem cavalry would appear out of nowhere, circle around the mobile Crusader host, release its volley of arrows and vanish, only to reappear a short time later with its quivers replenished.

In these circumstances the safety of the Crusader knight depended on his mail, helmet and shield. The arrows did not easily pierce his helmet and shield or penetrate the chain-rings of the mail, unless they struck at some vulnerable point like the neck or face. The development of the coat-of-mail and the helmet soon made even these targets rather difficult to reach. But this did not prevent the Moslems from shooting the horses out from under the mounted knights. A dismounted knight was no knight at all. Not only was his pride pricked, but his military effectiveness was reduced to nil.

Very soon the crusaders answered the Moslem challenge by partially adopting the type of fighting à la turque. But this was not easy. The crusaders, who were not very flexible in their ways, fell back on native talent, and long before the appearance of the 'spahee' in the French army, the crusaders created native regiments called Turcoples (sons of the Turks) that copied the Seljuq Turks in armament and techniques of fighting. Swift horses, light armour, quiver and bow were their main characteristics. The original warriors may actually have been Turks or half-breed Turks and Byzantines, but ultimately they were recruited locally among the native population, like Armenians or Bedouin, and later on possibly even among the Crusader natives, that is the Poulains. These troops did not fight in the actual Crusader battles, but they were much appreciated as reconnaissance units, though their main task was to repel the sudden attacks of the Seljuq Turks and prevent them from exploiting the advantage of the bow and arrow. The military orders also had their own regiments of Turcoples, and a special officer was detached to recruit and command them.

Successful as the use of the Turcople regiments might have been, the crusaders also reacted to the Turkish challenge by inventing an original way of fighting based on the rehabilitation of the common archer. Two hundred years before the longbows of the Welshmen decided English battles against French knights, the crusaders introduced foot archers as an integral part of their hosts. Whereas in twelfth century Europe the bow and arrow were relegated to the domain of hunting or were left to the commoners as a rather despised way of fighting, the crusaders created archer contingents for their hosts. Lightly equipped with an iron or leather cap, jerkins, a wooden shield, pike, bow and arrows, the archers became the front-line fighters of the host.

Marching before the contingents of mounted knights, at their flanks and rear, they were responsible for keeping the enemy at a respectable distance and preventing the Seljuq mounted archers from using their weapons effectively. In ranged battles they served as a protective wall behind which the knights massed until the time and position were propitious. Once they released their arrows, they would open up ranks and let the charge of the heavy Crusader cavalry move against the enemy. The archers were recruited among the burgesses, that is the non-noble Franks, and normally it was the duty of the cities and ecclesiastical institutions to furnish archer contingents to the host. These were the *serjeants à pied*, some of whom also fought as contingents of light cavalry, the *serjeants à cheval*.

The ingenious use of the foot archer on the march and in battle depended on the preservation of disciplined order among the various formations. This was a difficult problem in every medieval army, with its unbridled nobles. The young bloods, intent upon proving themselves and decorating themselves with glory in the eyes of their comrades, were never easily mastered. The problem was even more difficult in the Crusaders armies, as the pace of march and the momentum of attack were in great measure dictated by the slow-moving archers and pikemen. This hampered the movement of the knights, and in the face of the enemy it was not easy to curb the martial ardour of the warriors, especially those who had come all the way from Europe to fight the Infidel. Yet it was discipline, at least in the sense of not breaking the ranks of the archers, on which the safety of the whole host depended.

The enemy soon discovered the soft spot in the Crusader formations. As far as possible, the Moslems evaded any head-on encounter with the crusaders, for the chances were that they would be swept away by the whirlwind of the heavy iron cavalry. This meant avoiding battles on open plains, which allowed the effective use of heavy cavalry, and the Moslems preferred the advantage in hilly, mountainous or broken terrain. On the other hand, they manoeuvred to strike a wedge and separate the foot archers from the Crusader cavalry. Once separated, the Crusader mounted knights were stripped of archer protection and thus a target for the arrows of Turkish cavalry. The Moslems had learned their lessons well. This manoeuvre was the major reason for the defeat of the Crusader armies at the fatal battle of Hittin.

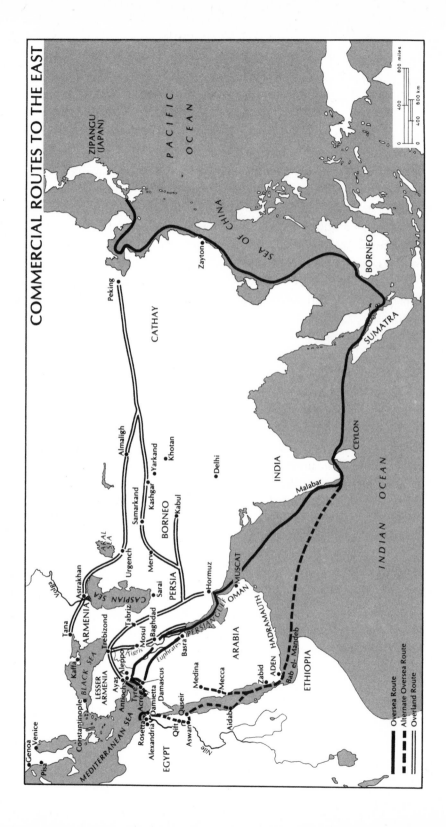

COMMERCIAL ROUTES TO THE EAST

Oversea Route
Alternate Oversea Route
Overland Route

PACIFIC OCEAN

ZIPANGU (JAPAN)

SEA OF CHINA

BORNEO

SUMATRA

Peking

CATHAY

Zayton

CEYLON

INDIA

Malabar

INDIAN OCEAN

Almaligh

Yarkand

Khotan

Delhi

Samarkand

Kashgar

Kabul

BORNEO

Merv

Urgench

Sarai

PERSIA

Hormuz

MUSCAT

GULF OF OMAN

PERSIAN GULF

ARAL SEA

Volga

Astrakhan

CASPIAN SEA

Tana

ARMENIA

Trebizond

Tabriz

Mosul

Baghdad

Basra

Tigris

Euphrates

Medina

Mecca

ARABIA

HADRAMAUTH

ADEN

Bab el-Mandeb

Zabid

ETHIOPIA

Aidab

Genoa

Venice

Pisa

Constantinople

BLACK SEA

Kaffa

LESSER ARMENIA

Aleppo

Ayas

Antioch

Tyre

Acre

Damascus

Rosetta

Alexandria

Damietta

Qift

Quseir

Aswan

Nile

EGYPT

MEDITERRANEAN SEA

800 miles

400

800 km

400

9

The Adventure of Commerce and the Expanding Universe

If one is intent upon landing in the aforesaid city of Acre, let him sail at a distance of three miles from the Church of St Andrew, because of the reef which is at the height of that church. Let him then sail straight until he sees beyond the 'Tower of the Flies' the house which was once of the constable, and then he can turn into the port. And when he enters the aforesaid port, let him sail therein in such a way that the castle of Haifa or Porphyria remains in the middle of the stern, all the time holding the 'Tower of the Flies' at the middle of the prow of the ship. And keeping to these directions, he will safely sail into the port.

Such were the instructions given in a thirteenth-century navigation manual to ships approaching the Levantine coast. The moment a ship was seen on the horizon on the final run of the three-week journey from Italy, the sentinels in the 'Tower of the Flies' or on the citadel's battlements signalled their superiors, church bells began ringing and the representatives of the ship's nationals and a good many of the city's inhabitants made their way to the port area. The vivid colours of the painted ships, so beloved by medieval captains, were topped by masts and floating flags of St Mark, St Peter or St Lawrence, patron saints of the Italian maritime powers, together with white banners bearing the red cross, which proclaimed Crusaders' faith and commercial privileges. The arrival of the ship, or normally of the *stola*, that is an entire convoy, was a feast day, a field-day for the innkeeper, merchant and everyone else in the city. Pilgrims, relatives and business associates carrying news from home, were soon to disembark at the city's inner port. Merchandise, assignations, bills of exchange, bills of credit – all the paraphernalia of commerce – would soon change hands and be injected into the commercial arteries of the city. One could often see as many as a hundred ships in the confined space of the ports of Tyre, Acre and even the insecure and rocky port of Jaffa. The larger ships could carry a thousand merchants and pilgrims in addition to some five hundred tons of cargo.

Merchandise was unloaded over ladders or planks on the backs of porters, often Euro-Asians, called 'Poulains of the port' to the cluttered quays of the extremely narrow port area. This area was almost always characterised by an overpowering stench, because the beach was the normal drainage and garbage outlet of the city and slaughter-houses and skinners' and tanners' workshops were located there. Once their goods were unloaded, merchants went through the traditional Levantine custom of haggling with the customs authorities. Nothing could be more confused and complicated than medieval customs duties, particularly in the Crusader ports. Not only did the customs vary with the type of merchandise, but there were different duties according to the goods' place of origin and the nationality of the ship and merchant. The same merchandise transported on the same ship would be subject to anything between 2% and 15% customs duties according to the nationality of the ship and its owner.

Where there are customs, there is smuggling, false declarations of value and, above all, false declarations of nationals' identity. Identification was often an intelligent guess, and bribery of port officials very often paid off in the form of duty exemptions. A major obligation of the colonial officials of the communes was to ensure that their respective nationals – Venetians, Genoese, Pisans and others – would fully enjoy their exemption privileges. Still, merchants from Tuscany often declared themselves to be Pisans, Catalans or nationals of Barcelona in order to profit from the exemptions of the communes. Though regulations were strict, their enforcement was almost impossible.

Once the haggling over customs duties was over, merchant and merchandise made their way to the fondaci or factories, the Crusader equivalents of the oriental caravanserais, of the city. These were located as close to the docks as possible. As everywhere else, the port area was the 'red district' of the city, though prostitutes were to be found even in the closely guarded factories of the communes and even in houses rented (for ruinously high rents) by clerics, notwithstanding the fulminations of the Roman pontiff. A square market or a long and

opposite Risks and profits in Mediterranean commerce. The odyssey of a Spanish merchant ship on its way to Crusader Acre, from a 13th-century Spanish illuminated manuscript

Como un meirador fu en sa naue a acre roueegin terinta

Eprometeu la offerta boa a s.ñ de salas ta terinta qdou logo.

Como chegaron á acre r foron muy ledos p en

Como uento en muy ton todas sas meirhadias ganega

Como se goinar a sa terra saos r con saure r con ganea.

Como compriu sa romaria a salas reuon y las offertas

narrow street, flanked by buildings several stories high, with magazines and shops on the ground level and lodgings on the upper floors, was the heart of the commune's establishment. These were cities within cities. They had their own church, bakery and baths. There were stables for horses, mules and camels and watering places (*sibils*) for man and beast. The largest building, three or four stories high, was the *palazzo* and residence of the viscount or consul of the commune. This was also the seat of the council where justice was dispensed according to the laws of Venice, Genoa, Pisa, Amalfi, Marseilles or Barcelona. The flag of the commune over the *palazzo* proclaimed its political and jurisdictional autonomy. Some *palazzi* were equipped with dark dungeons where prisoners were kept and sometimes executed.

Though some of the communal quarters had their own food-markets, the great commercial centre, the *fonde* or market-place, belonged to the lord of the city. In a large city like Jerusalem, whatever was saleable concentrated in specialised markets. Customs were paid on food entering the city at the city gates, in the Tower of David, but additional taxes were paid by buyer and seller negotiating their bargains. Dry and liquid measures and weights and balances were determined (for a fee) by market officials, the *plazzearii*, who were supervised by the *mathesep*, or market inspector. The grain market, which catered to the man, his mount and often his poultry and sheep, was a huge open space where wheat, barley, oats, spelt and so on were offered by the Moslem and oriental Christian *fellaheen*. In Jerusalem, this grain market at Jaffa Gate was in the vicinity of the pigsty and pork market, whereas sheep and beef were sold near the Temple area. Surely enough, butchers, skinners and tanners settled here to be near their sources of supply and at the same time near the natural drainage area of the city, the Valley of Josaphat, into which they poured the polluted water and the urine used in their trade.

The pride of every city was its bazaars. The markets of Jerusalem, Acre and Tyre were high, vaulted structures, where the different trades divided up the confined area of the shops. The merchant and craftsman displayed their merchandise at the open doors which faced on the street and its milling throngs of potential buyers. The vaulted ceilings or cloth strung over the street protected the shoppers against the sun and rain, but kept the market in quasi-darkness. The din of bidding and bargaining in every language under the sun and the pungent smells of spices were mixed with the acrid effluvium of kitchen-stalls in the so-called 'Street of Bad Cooking'. These open kitchen-stalls were characteristic of Crusader cities. Oriental in origin, they proved to be extremely practical in places visited by an ever changing flood of piligrims, just as they corresponded to the needs in a country where (in the beginning at least) a large portion of the population was composed of bachelors.

Near its market-places, almost every large city had a street or area inhabited by money-changers. This was a typical burgher's occupation which in Europe was practised at international fairs or maritime cities, but in the Holy Land it was an everyday necessity because of the influx of crusaders, pilgrims and merchants from the four corners of Europe. Here in the 'change' and its row of benches (banchi), European money was exchanged for local currency. To deal with the innumerable and confusing varieties of coinage from hundreds of European mints, assess their intrinsic metal value and convert them into the corresponding local currency was a trying experience. One has only to remember that European coinage – for example, the French – was constantly being debased by the government (this is the medieval equivalent of devaluation) or 'shaved' or counterfeited by local merchants. It goes without saying that every pilgrim felt himself cheated in the exchange.

In addition, money-changers had to deal not only with European coinage but also with that of the Near East. The standard currency of the country before the Crusader conquest was the Egyptian, Fatimid gold *dinar* and the silver *dirhem*. These mingled, especially in the maritime cities, with the currencies of Moslem Syria, Mesopotamia and even distant Persia. Large amounts of such currency, if not hoarded, came into Frankish mints through taxes, but they also remained in circulation after the conquest. Frankish mints tried even to imitate, albeit clumsily, the Moslem coinage. Consequently, the exchange of Moslem and Frankish coinage was a daily occurrence even for routine business. On the other hand, commercial relations with the neighbouring Moslem countries were never entirely interrupted, even in times of war and siege, and they flourished during times of peace. This situation, as well as maritime commerce with North Africa, brought Moslem currency into circulation. To it we may add currency brought with the pilgrimages of oriental Christians, Jews and Moslems. Thus a Crusader money-changer was a go-between for European and non-European currencies. To deal with their problems efficiently, money-changers tended to specialise. In Jerusalem, for example, one street was taken up by Frankish money-changers, whereas their counterparts on the other side of the bazaars were the 'Syrian' money-changers, oriental Christians who probably specialised in oriental currency.

In time the crusaders struck their own gold, silver and copper coins. The Crusader gold coin was called the *Saracen besant*, a reminder that the first gold coins the Europeans came across were of Byzantine origin, whereas the gold coins in circulation in their own colonies were those of the neighbouring Islamic states. Soon after, the crusaders began imitating the Moslem *dinar* and *dirhem*. In time, the early clumsy imitations improved, but their quality remained inferior to both the Byzantine and Moslem originals in weight and especially alloy. It is doubtful whether this type of Crusader coinage fooled any professional merchant as to its real value, but it was nonetheless accepted in the international trade of the Mediterranean. Moreover, Syrian Crusader coinage became the standard in dealings with the natives of the country. At the same time, the crusaders struck their own coins of silver and copper modelled after contemporary French currency. In addition to the name of the reigning king on the rim and the cross in the middle, on the reverse side such coins bore an image of the Tower of David or of the ruling king. The most curious Crusader coins were those struck after the middle of the thirteenth century on which the Arabic inscription praised the Holy Trinity! This was a practical solution allowing a Christian mint to proclaim its faith without perjury and sacrilege and still to profit from the international market.

Busy as they were, the local markets and bazaars mainly catered to the immediate needs of the local population. This situation had existed in Palestine and Syria before the coming of the crusaders. But their conquest added a new dimension to the economic life of the country, and its historical importance lay far beyond their precarious frontiers.

It would be no exaggeration to state that the period of the Crusades coincided with the first great explorations of the inhabited globe. The impulse to explore the unknown was not the direct result of the Crusades, but they were instrumental in creating the physical and psychological conditions for this first outburst of exploration, three hundred years before the great Age of Discoveries. The heroes of the latter turned west and south, spanning the Atlantic Ocean. But it should not be forgotten that they wanted to reach the same goals which had been reached by merchants, explorers and missionaries in their travels three centuries earlier during the age of the Crusades.

At the beginning of the twelfth century, direct commerce with the Levant and, through its bases, with the coasts of northern and eastern Africa and even with Central Asia and the Far East (albeit less common) was not a rarity. Merchants and sailors from Southern Europe maintained communications links with the great markets of the Levant. The most frequented one, Constantinople, besides having its own marvellous products, was a major terminal of the great commerical routes on the north–south axis, from Scandinavia to the Levant (and eventually Africa) and the east–west axis from the Far East to the Mediterranean. Competing in importance with Byzantium were Alexandria and, between these two, a large number of smaller ports, like Damietta and Antioch.

In the early Middle Ages, Amalfi and Venice were the main European cities which mediated between Catholic Europe, Orthodox Byzantium and the world of Islam. One of the major features of this early commercial activity was the fact that the European merchants could not penetrate beyond the terminals of commerce. The Byzantine *apothecai*, like the Moslem *funduqs* in the maritime cities and road terminals, were as far as one could go, and any place beyond those points was 'out of bounds' for aliens. This allowed the local powers to control exports and imports, prices, taxes and customs duties and, above all, to preserve the monopoly over the great international trade routes for their nationals and privileged merchants.

The invisible but solid wall which barred Europe from the main sources of supply broke down during the age of the Crusades. By the twelfth century, the European merchant no longer waited in Constantinople, Antioch or Acre, nor even Alexandria or Damietta, for the arrival of camel caravans or ships loaded with merchandise. They had already found their way into the nearby hinterland – be it Damascus, Baghdad or Armenia – and by the thirteenth century, following the creation of the Euro-Asian empire of the Mongols, they reached the limits of the Euro-Asian continent, sailed into the Indian Ocean and even reached the marvellous spice islands beyond Indochina. The *oikumene*, the inhabited world of the Greeks (which for a short time, with the phalanx of Alexander the Great, reached the confines of India), burst its restraining boundaries, opening up (albeit ephemerally) an entire continent. What triggered off this tremendous '*Drang nach Osten*' was the lure of profit. There were some vague attempts at global diplomacy, and missionary efforts to spread Christianity were not entirely absent, but it would be fitting to preface the story of the medieval expanding universe with the inscription on the title page of an Italian account book: 'In the name of God and profit'!

First to be reached were the great emporia of the Mediterranean. How they impressed contemporaries can be gauged by quoting the great Crusader historian William of Tyre:

> Alexandria has the reputation of receiving a larger supply of wares of every description than any other maritime city. Whatever our world lacks in spices, pearls, oriental treasures and foreign wares is brought hither from the two Indies, Saba, Arabia, even from both the Ethiopias and from Persia and other lands nearby. Thus masses of people from East and West flock thither, making Alexandria the public mart of both worlds.

A contemporary of William of Tyre, Benjamin of Tudela, was far more accustomed to great and flourishing cities in his native Moslem Spain; but he can hardly find words to describe Constantinople:

> Merchants of every description come here from the lands of Babylon, all the territories of Shin'ar and of Persia, Media and all the kingdoms of Egypt. They come also from the land of Canaan [probably lands of the Slavs] and the kingdom of Russia [Kiev], from Hungary, the land of the Petchenegs, from the land of Khazaria [Crimea] and the land of Lombardy and Spain. It is a bustling city, and merchants traffic in it from every country, coming there by sea and by land, and there is none like it in the whole world excepting Baghdad, the great city of Ismael.

Similar descriptions of other great emporia of the Levant could be easily gathered from contemporary sources. Yet few Europeans ever penetrated beyond the artificial walls of these commercial centres. Everybody knew that the great riches and the incredible variety of merchandise was not produced locally, that it came from the south and the east. Sometimes the places of origin of the different articles were known, but very little else. Wider knowledge was to be found among the practical people engaged in transport and commerce, rather than among the scholars. For the latter, as well as for the early medieval cartographers, somewhere to the east was Paradise. Adam and Eve, modestly covering their nude bodies, take up the upper corner of medieval maps (the upper corner points east according to medieval usage). Often two of the four rivers mentioned in Genesis 2, 10 spring from the place, disappear in the soil and miraculously reappear again as the Tigris and Euphrates; and whereas there is some confusion as to which of the other two rivers (Pishon and Gihon) was which, there is no doubt that the Nile was one of them and the Ganges was sometimes identified with the other. The more literally minded drew a flame and cherubim near this Paradise (Genesis 3, 24), or cut it off from the inhabited earth by mountains, flames and desert. Only Alexander the Great (according to one of the versions of his medieval romance), having conquered India, came to a city where he was instructed by a Jew that this was the Terrestrial Paradise!

The age of the Crusades, however, witnessed the disappearance of the *apothekai* at the road terminals and the Byzantine *mitata, xenodochia* or caravanserais, in which a foreign merchant was tolerated and supervised during his prescribed and limited stay. Now the *fondachi* from Constantinople through Christian Armenia, the Crusader establishments and even Moslem Alexandria assured for merchants both lodgings and the necessary local and foreign contacts. Some time later, these merchants would be found in Aleppo, Damascus and Baghdad, at the terminals of the Asian sea and land routes, and thereafter at Trebizond, Kaffa and Tana on the Black Sea. By then the spice roads would no longer be a mystery, and the first Europeans would reach India, China and the islands of Indonesia. For a whole century, Asia would be linked to Europe and the veil of mystery, which surrounded it since the barbarians overran Europe in the sixth century, would be lifted. But this achievement was short-lived, and a hundred years later Asia was again shrouded in darkness for the Europeans, waiting to be rediscovered by Italians, Spaniards and Portuguese in the sixteenth century.

Nothing could better express the excitement of expanding horizons than the opening page of the greatest travel memoir of the Middle Ages, or perhaps of any age, dictated by a prisoner in a Genoese goal in 1298 to a fellow-prisoner, Rusticello of Pisa: 'From the creation of Adam to the present day, no man, whether pagan, or Saracen, or Christian or other, of whatever progeny or generation he may have been, ever saw or inquired into so many and such great things.' Thus Marco Polo invites his audience to read about 'the diversities of the races of mankind, as well as the diversities of kingdoms, provinces, and regions of all parts of the East ... the most marvellous characteristics of the peoples especially in Armenia, Persia, India and Tartary'. But Marco Polo was not the first to penetrate the limitless stretches of

Asia. By 1245 a Christian embassy had already travelled to the East in the hope of concluding an alliance with the Mongols against Islam. Giovanni of Piano Carpini (1245), André of Longumeau (1249) and William of Rubruquis (1251) preceded Marco Polo's voyage. But it is the latter whose name is celebrated down through history for acquainting Europe with the marvellous East.

What drove Europeans eastwards can be summarised in one word: spices. The medieval meaning of the word was far wider than that of modern times. It included not only seasonings, perfumes, dye-stuffs and medicinals of the Orient, but almost every type of import from Africa and the East. A thirteenth-century writer, Huon de Méry, describes a merchant as '*vendeur d'épices et de denrées exotiques*', and this is probably the closest one can come to the medieval definition of the generic term 'spices'. Some three hundred spices are named in a fourteenth-century mercantile manual. Their use in European life was not entirely unknown in the early Middle Ages. But by the time of the Crusades, spices, while neither a luxury item nor common in Europe, were enough in demand to drive the wheels of European economic life for centuries.

Dye-stuffs were needed in the great textile centres of northern Italy and for the looms of Flanders, smaller centres in France, Germany and England. These colourants were a primary necessity that was only partially supplied from local sources, and those were usually not of the best quality. Other 'spices' included perfumes and every type of incense. In this the type of oriental ware, reminiscences of classical antiquity and the Bible conjointly created images that have survived up to modern times. The clientele of perfumes were not exclusively female. Contrary to popular belief, medieval men including ecclesiastics, used perfume, evidenced by the fact that Palestinian clergy visiting the court of Henry II of England were severely rebuked because of the cloud of perfume in which they seemed to be surrounded.

In the stricter meaning of the word, spices included herbs, aromatic herbs or extracts of plants, and fruits or their juices used as condiments or as an ingredient of sauces. One of the important tasks of spices, however, was the preservation of food for long periods. Some spices, pepper probably being the most important, were used as often as condiments as preservatives. From here it was only a small step to the medieval pharmacopoeia, often a mixture of ancient knowledge, classical and medieval lore and empirical observation. Even the most exotic spices were quite prominent in the druggists' stock, which lacked neither gold nor silver among its items. Considering the high prices of spices, one can imagine the cost of the medicaments.

Textiles, especially sumptuous ones, held a place close to spices in commerce with the Orient. Naturally, Flanders and somewhat later England, as well as northern Italy, were great textile producers; but it was the Orient which flooded the West with exorbitant products. Despite the fact that cotton and linen textiles were produced in Europe, the quality, and often the finish, of Eastern products easily found a market in the West. And it was the sumptuous textiles of the Orient, with a relatively restrained circle of consumers, which gave oriental commerce a special atmosphere: silks of finest quality, and even more so ornamented fabrics of silk; brocades using gold and silver threads; the 'baldechino' (its name pointing to Baghdad origin); damask (from Damascus); samite from Greece or Byzantium; taffeta from Persia; satin from Zayton, that is Tsuen-tcheou-fou in the Chinese province of Fo-Kien; and cheaper textiles like the buckram from Bokhara, camelot (originally from camel hair) and the like were exotic to the eye and touch alike. It was not only the superiority of the primary materials, but the marvellous workmanship of designers and weavers which helped oriental textiles and the rich colours – blues, reds, purples, greens – penetrate church sacristies and royal, princely and patrician wardrobes. Accompanying the fabrics was jewellery and precious stones from the Orient, although in this field the West sold coral to the East.

The exotic products, natural and fabricated, invoked the strange-sounding names of distant lands. A contemporary historian wrote that paralleling the Illiad of the crusading knights was an Odyssey of the merchants – but even more so of merchandise. From the Far East, Marco Polo's island of Zipangu (Japan) and the Javas (Borneo and Sumatra), Cathay, Tartary and Indochina, the merchandise usually travelled through the longer, but cheaper and usually safer, sea route, changing ships, crews and merchants several times until it reached the shores of the Mediterranean. Chinese sailors and merchants, using large sea-going vessels which had evoked Marco Polo's admiration, brought goods to Ceylon or to Malabar on the south-western coast of India, where Indian sailors and merchants took over. They sailed westwards through the Indian Ocean, often referred to at this time as the Arabian Sea. Their maritime course to the West either took the

Hierosolyma became al-Quds (The Holy). A rosace from a Crusader church adorns a Mameluk fountain near the entrance to the Temple esplanade at the Gate of the Chain in Jerusalem (91)

After the fall of the kingdom attempts were made to eradicate all traces of the Crusader rule. Baybars used church portals to support a bridge between Ramle and Lydda, the birth-place of St George. His heraldic leopards crush the cornered Crusader rat (92)

Expelled from the mainland, crusaders clung to the nearby Mediterranean islands in the hope of a future *reconquista*. The Order of St John moved to Cyprus and then to Rhodes. Its navy challenged Moslem power, and the island-turned-fortress withstood Mameluk and Ottoman assaults. Rhodes besieged by the Ottoman Turks (93)

overleaf The siege of Rhodes by the Ottomans. The immense camp of the Turks surrounds the crumbling fortifications of the city and its knightly defenders. With the fall of Rhodes (1522), the knights moved to Malta, where they remained a sovereign order until expelled by Napoleon in 1798 (94)

direction of Hormuz and the Persian Gulf or continued westwards to Aden in the Arabian peninsula. The first route, if not impeded by pirates in the Persian Gulf, would then continue northwards to the delta of the Euphrates at the head of the gulf. But this short route was often abandoned because pirates working out of small insular bases infested the entrance to the Persian Gulf. So it was at the entrance to the gulf that the Indian ships unloaded their wares and smaller ships with Persian or Arab crews took over. The sea route ended in Basra, the main port of southern Iraq. Here the merchandise was again unloaded and transferred to river boats able to navigate the Tigris River to Baghdad. Baghdad or Damascus were normally the terminal stations of the Eastern routes. European merchants would contract their business there and transport their purchases on camels to Antioch, Tyre, Acre or Ayas (in Lesser Armenia). Sometimes Moslem merchants or oriental Christians like the 'Massorini' (merchants of Mosul) would frequent the Christian ports of the Crusader establishments and might even have maintained branches of their companies there. Then the precious wares of the Orient made the last leg of their journey to Europe. European vessels would load the precious cargo from its transit stations in the Crusader establishments and, God and winds willing, would arrive three to five weeks later in Venice, Pisa or Genoa.

The second maritime route branched off from the Indian Ocean and, instead of sailing into the Persian Gulf, contoured the coast of Muscat, Oman and Hadramauth to unload at Aden or even sail through the strait of Bab el-Mandeb between Arabia and Ethiopia and unload at Zabid. This was the terminal of the Indian deep-sea vessels. Here the cargo would change ships and crews for the lighter vessels of the Red Sea before proceeding northwards. The islands, reefs and shallow waters of the Red Sea demanded ships of smaller tonnage and pilots familiar with the dangers of the waters. It is here that merchant vessels met the pilgrim vessels which made their way to Yanbu and Jedda, the ports of Medina and Mecca. The cargo-laden ships sailed northwards to the Egyptian ports of 'Aidab or Quseir, whence they were transported by camel caravans across the desert to the first Nile cataract at Aswan or further north to Qift. Here the Nile barges carried the cargo downstream, manoeuvring into one of the river's tributaries which ended at Damietta, Rosetta or, most important, Alexandria. From here European ships brought the wares to the ports of southern Europe.

Though this was the safest and most frequented route, there was

a third East–West commercial axis – a land route over the steppes and
deserts of Central Asia – which transported oriental wares from the
Far East to the West on camel back. Its terminals in the West were
Kaffa in the Crimea, Tana and Trebizond on the shore of the Black
Sea, Constantinople and Ayas in Lesser Armenia. From these terminals
the Italian merchants started out on the long journey to the shores of the
Sea of China. Whereas the maritime route took almost two years, the
overland route was shorter, some nine months in all. Though the road –
often called the 'Silk Road' to stress its major attraction – was known
since ancient times, its use by Europeans became practical only with
with the establishment and pacification of the great Mongol Empire
(*c.* 1250). Then, as noted in an Italian manual of commerce, one could
pass over the vast stretches in perfect safety both by day and by night.

Few European products were directly exported to the Far East in
exchange for the precious silk. The normal practice was to exchange
European products for local ones along the route. Basically there were
two main roads leading to the East, a northern and a southern one, the
latter also branching off to the Arabian Sea or India. Merchants often
ended their eastern voyage in Sarai on the Volga, Astrakhan on the
Caspian Sea or Urgench near the Aral Sea; others did not venture
beyond Tabriz in Persia. The more adventurous or enterprising crossed
the Mongol frontier to the east of the Black Sea and continued through
Astrakhan and Urgench to Almaligh and thence to Peking. The
southern direction from Ayas and Tabriz contoured the southern coast
of the Caspian Sea and then through Merv, Bokhara, Samarkand and
Kashgar, continuing to Yarkand, Khotan and Peking, unless one
chose to turn to Kabul and reach the Moslem state in India, with its
capital at Delhi.

Crusades, Italian daring and skill and Mongolian invasion, three
very different factors, created a constellation which laid the foundations
of Euro-Asian contacts. To medieval man, who had an acute feeling of
the marvellous, the new world which he perceived in a fog of description, together with the tangible proofs of its existence in the form of the
oriental wares, was one more of God's marvels. True, there were
sceptics, but very often for the wrong reasons. When Marco Polo
was pressed to avow on his deathbed that the narrative of his journey
was full of fables, he could only answer that he had not told even one-
half of what he had really lived and seen.

10

Epilogue

'Before the end of the world, all prophecies have to be fulfilled; the Gospels need be diffused all over the world and the Holy City of Jerusalem has to be given back to the Christian Church.' This was not written by a mystic or would-be prophet of the Middle Ages; it was written by Christopher Columbus, the Italian navigator in the service of Their Majesties, the Most Catholic Kings of Spain, after the discovery of the New World. His caravels carried white sails with red crosses, the traditional sign of the crusaders, and on the deck of one of his ships was a converted Jew, Luis de Torres, as an interpreter of Arabic!

About two hundred years elapsed between the fall of Acre and the discovery of the New World. The crusading idea, though weakened, was not dead. The antagonism between West and East did not disappear, and the notion of a Holy War had not been abandoned. But more and more, circumstances changed the notion of the Holy War from an offensive against Islam into a war to defend the True Faith against the encroaching powers of Islam. For one, Islam was no longer represented only by Arab-ruled states, but by the great Ottoman Empire. Master of Constantinople (renamed Istanbul) from 1453, the Turkish Empire was far more dangerous than its predecessors.

The fall of Acre, which sealed the fate of the Latin kingdom, did not erase all the territorial acquisitions of the Crusades. There was the vigorous kingdom of Cyprus ruled by the Lusignans, descendants of the kings of Jerusalem; the Christian kingdom of Armenia in Asia Minor, which, though neither founded nor settled by the crusaders, owed its creation and to some degree its courtly culture to the Frankish states in the East; the islands of the Aegean, some part of the maritime empire of Venice and others ruled by Frankish dynasties in the wake of the Fourth Crusade; and, finally, the island of Rhodes, captured and ruled from the beginning of the fourteenth century by the knights of St John. Pushed off the mainland, the crusaders clung to its fringes on a maritime cordon which divided Asia from Europe.

Throughout the fourteenth century, the feeling remained that a new crusade would move out of Europe and, wisened by earlier experience and chastised by former mistakes, would strike a fatal blow to Islam. In this perspective, the islands in the eastern Mediterranean appeared as bridgeheads and stepping stones to the conquest of the Holy Land. The confidence was stregthened and reinforced by a new literary genre: '*De recuperatione Terrae Sanctae*' – On the Recovery of the Holy Land. Since the Second Church Council at Lyons in 1274, when Pope Gregory X commissioned suggestions on how to save the Crusader kingdom, a bountiful crop of such plans had been pouring into the Roman curia and royal chanceries throughout Europe. Some of the plans were pure chimerical fantasies combining Bible and theology with wishful thinking; others, more sober, drew conclusions from history, even recent Crusader history, combined with an excellent knowledge of commerce, its impact, needs and routes, and evaluations of the military potential of the Moslem antagonists. These were not merely arguments in the hands of polemists and propagandists; they directly influenced the thinking of statesmen and generals. In the new web of political and commercial relations, the recovery of the Holy Land was a pressing need. Often the desire to do so was no more than a kind of cultural convention. But more often it was accompanied by the sincere belief that military and economic means would ultimately reach their goal.

In the end, the large number of theoretical projects and practical preparation gave rise to only two expeditions which might be called crusades. One was led by Peter I Lusignan, king of Cyprus (1365); the other was the Crusade of Nicopolis (1396). Both are characteristic of the fourteenth century. Peter I, who tried (with the help of the papacy) to mobilise the West for a new crusade, visited Venice, Avignon, Strasbourg, Paris, Rouen, London, Prague and Cracow. Doge, pope, emperor and the kings of France, England, Poland and Hungary received the gallant king, whose renown was enhanced by fighting the Turks on the coast of Asia Minor with greatest honour. The results were not entirely disappointing, and the forces assembled were impressive. But it was the spirit of chivalry, rather than political thinking, which animated the expedition.

Concentrated in Cyprus, the Crusader fleet was launched against Alexandria (9 October 1365). The city was taken by storm, and there followed two days of thorough looting, which spared not even the Christian quarters. A week later, though, with the approach of the Moslem armies from Cairo, king, knight and foot soldier left the smouldering city for the safety of their ships. This was the end of the expedition which gave vent to the chivalrous aspirations of European knighthood, but was more an act of piracy than a crusade.

At the time Peter I of Cyprus was burning the gates of Alexandria, Europe was ever more seriously menaced by the Ottoman Turks. From their base near Dorylaeum (Eskisehir), the site of the First Crusade's greatest victory, the Turks quickly reached the shores of the Bosporus, the Aegean and the Black Sea. At the death of Osman (1326), they were masters of Brussa and Nicaea, the city hallowed by the first ecumenical council in Church history. Soon Anatolia in the interior and Aydin on the shores of the Mediterranean were Turkish, and in the second half of the century the Turks invaded and captured Thrace. Rumelia and Bulgaria, as well as parts of Macedonia. It was now Islam which took the initiative, penetrating Europe through the Balkans. Cyprus, Rhodes, the islands of the Aegean and the lands of the Slavs and Hungarians were directly threatened. The pope tried, in vain, to create a Christian coalition in the name of a crusade. And as history will have its reversals and ironies, the crusade now became a war of defence against the aggressive Infidel. But the only tangible result of the papal appeals was the ill-fated expedition preached by Pope Boniface IX and led by John, duke of Burgundy. French, German, English, Valachs, and Czechs participated in the campaign which descended the Danube from Buda to face the Turkish army of Bayazid in a pitched battle at Nicopolis (September 1396). The battle ended in disaster and the annihilation of the Christian army. Ultimately it was not a crusade or the Christian armies which stopped the Ottoman conquests, but the appearance of the formidable Timurlane, the founder of the second Mongol empire, who paralysed the Turks for a whole generation and put off their capture of Constantinople until 1453.

The battle of Nicopolis was the last great Christian expedition against Islam. Europe turned a deaf ear to those who tried to put a new crusade into motion. The climate of public opinion was definitely adverse to the enterprise. There were many reasons for the decline in enthusiasm for the Crusades. First and foremost was disappointment, even despair, over the failure of the movement. Tremendous in scope, the Crusades had cost hundreds of thousands in lives and fortunes without producing lasting results. Moreover, by the later half of the thirteenth century, and even more so in the fourteenth century, the Crusades were already out of tune with developments in European life. The movement was created as the most representative expression of a dominant pan-Christian ideology typical of the turn of the eleventh century. A hundred years later, at the death of Innocent III, Europe was more Christian than before, but superimposed upon this common basis of faith and culture were the particularistic feudal monarchies, the immediate predecessors of national monarchies. In the middle of the thirteenth century, the two powers which embodied the idea of pan-Christianity, papacy and empire – the spitirual and temporal representative of Christian Europe – were locked in a struggle which reduced them both close to impotence. The feudal monarchies, which commanded men's loyalties, took a far more sober look at their immediate futures and found them not to be in the grandiose 'res Christiana' but in the strengthening of their national states. The Latin establishments in the East were something to be proud of, but one did little to assure their survival. The Crusader states never created a nationality of their own, and in the thirteenth century they were as anachronistic as the movement which brought them into being.

But not only political and economic factors put an end to the Crusades. No less important, at least in circles which one would today described as 'intellectual', was the criticism and the growing opposition opposition to the Crusades as an *ideology*. Voices of opposition were heard as far back as the Second Crusade, and each succeeding expedition brought on a new wave of disillusionment and criticism. The many who opposed the Crusades ranged from the light-hearted and impudent troubadours to political thinkers, who deplored the exploitation of the movement for papal interests (for example, the campaign against Frederick II), and even mystics and men of profound faith and piety, who expressed doubts as to the divine inspiration of the movement because bloodshed was opposed to evangelical teachings. It is in these circles that a new idea arose: to preach the Gospels to the Infidels and thereby bring them to conversion. This new ideology of a peaceful mission inflamed the imagination, and it soon rivalled that of the Crusades.

As far back as the middle of the twelfth century, the great abbot of

Cluny, Peter the Venerable, had the Koran translated into Latin and so made it accessible to the West so as to serve the understanding of Islam and as a solid basis of anti-Islamic polemics. Some toyed with the idea that since the Prophets and Jesus were not rejected by Islam, it would be sufficient to point out the errors of Mohammed in order to bring Moslems into the fold of Christianity. Missions to the Mongols in the middle of the thirteenth century were essentially religious missions with the aim of converting the new power to Christianity. It was the Catalan Raymond Lull who, at the turn of the thirteenth century, became the most eloquent apostle of the missionary idea. Under his influence, the Council of Vienna (1311) decided to establish six schools of oriental languages to train the future propagandists and missionaries. Dominicans and Franciscans reached uncharted areas of the globe, preaching, discussing, baptising and establishing small local communities. Though some of their exploits could be classified as thrilling the missions never became a mass movement. Nonetheless, their existence undermined the idea of the Crusades and furnished a theoretical basis for opposition or rejection.

Despite handicaps, the ideology of the Crusades continued to survive, but with time it fixed new aims and consequently new means of action. The major change took place at the end of the fourteenth century and became dominant after the middle of the fifteenth century, when the idea of the Crusades became linked with the great movement of exploration. It is not always easy to know how much of the new ideal was window-dressing and how much sincere. It seems that the movement of exploration drew its inspiration from different sources influenced and appealed to people on different levels.

The great movement of discoveries began at the beginning of the fifteenth century with Portuguese explorers who reached the Atlantic islands in the West and contoured the western coast of Africa in the South. The Infante Enriquez of Portugal was the moving spirit behind these hazardous enterprises, which in less than a hundred years had changed the destiny of man. The Portuguese explorations of the coast of Africa were, in a sense, a continuation of the *reconquista*, a transfer of the Holy War — now at its last stages in the Iberian Peninsula — into the neighbouring lands of Islam and paganism. It would be a misreading of history to assign exclusively missionary aims to these explorations or even to presume that conversion to Christianity was a dominant factor. Yet there is no doubt that the daring captains, explorers and even hard-bitten merchants did believe that there was a more sublime purpose to their enterprises than the search for Eldorado. The spiritual aspect of the expeditions was linked to the belief in the 'white man's burden' of spreading the Gospel throughout the inhabited world. These latter-day apostles were profoundly Christian, and conversion of the unbelievers and baptism of the pagans were viewed as an integral part of their undertakings. Characteristic of this feeling was the fact that after the discovery of the New World, Columbus signed his name as Christoferens, the bearer of the good tidings of Christ to the New World. This missionary aspect is present throughout the period of the Great Discoveries. Christopher Columbus, as well as Vasco da Gama and even the great empire-founder Albuquerque were conscious of it and viewed it as a part of their tasks.

Columbus's expedition and expectations were based partially on the erroneous beliefs about the size of the earth and the notion that sailing westwards, one would reach India directly. Out of these premises grew the notion of an attack on Islam through its back door, that is from the East. The legend of the kingdom of Presbyter John, alternately located in the East and in Africa, and the fantastic descriptions of his riches and military power led to the assumption that an eastern alliance would enable an attack on Islam from two directions.

When the error became obvious, the Crusader idea was phrased in economic terms, namely that direct contact with the Spice Islands and India would make Europe commercially independent of Egypt, while simultaneously undermining Egypt's main economic resources: the income from duties on international commerce which terminated its Asio-African course in the Nile delta. Europe never succeeded in realising this program, but it was realised by the Ottoman Turks after their conquest of Egypt (1517) and the deviation of commercial routes to their new capital in Istanbul. While this ruined Egypt, it spurred Europe to new exploratory efforts in order to break the Turkish monopoly on commerce with the Far East. Yet the domination of commerce with Asia, as well as the discovery of gold in the New World, still served the vision of the defunct Crusades. While sailing westwards and expanding the distances between the Christian world and the Holy Land, Columbus noted in his shipboard ledger: 'I propose to Your Majesties that all the profit to be derived from my enterprise should be used for the recovery of Jerusalem.'

Author's Note

The composition of *The World of the Crusaders* was guided by the desire to relate the story of the Crusades and to make the society created and sustained by them accessible to the wider reading public. The book was conceived as a balanced combination of narrative and pictorial commentary. Hence, almost without exception, the rich illustrative material is contemporary with the Crusades and their aftermath, which not only helps the reader visualise the material surroundings of the crusaders' existence, but often projects the crusaders' image of themselves. Some of the illustrations are simple records; others have intrinsic artistic value; still others represent tangible remains of a culture which flourished under Eastern skies some seven hundred years ago. The juxtaposition of illustrative material drawn from the Occident and the Orient, often depicting the same occasions, brings to life the meeting of East and West in the Crusader kingdom.

I would like to express my gratitude to a number of people who were associated with the preparation of this work. Miss Ina Friedman's enthusiasm, editorial guidance, knowledge and taste were of enormous help in shaping the contents of the book. Mrs Irène Lewitt gave valuable aid in the selection of photographs, and Mr Alex Berlyne's design and artistic layout are as intelligent as they are elegant. Finally, my thanks go to Mrs Dvora Keil, who prepared the index, and to my assistant, Miss Sylvia Schein, who was most helpful throughout the writing of the book.

Joshua Prawer

July 1972   Jerusalem

Picture Credits

The author and the publishers wish to thank the following institutions and individuals for their gracious cooperation, aid and permission to reproduce the illustrations appearing in this work: Bibliothèque Nationale, Paris, 1, 4, 8, 10, 13, 15, 20, 23, 24, 25, 27, 30, 37, 39, 42, 46, 52, 56, 57, 60, 61, 62, 65, 69, 79, 80, 82, 83, 86, 90, 93, 94, jacket illustrations, endpaper illustrations, opposite page 24, opposite page 48; David Harris, 11, 12, 38, 47, 55, 71, 76, 81, 87, 89, 91, 92, opposite page 64; El Escorial, 9, 41, 68, opposite page 136; Mas, Barcelona, 9, 41, 68, opposite page 136; L. A. Mayer Memorial Association, Jerusalem, 17, 26, 28, 40, 51, 85; Photo Hinz, 2, opposite page 8; Alinari, 5; Detroit Institute of Arts, 6; Musée des Monuments Français, 7, 36, 43, 63, 66; Israel Department of Antiquities, 14, 16, 22, 35, 38, 44, 78; Ronald Sheridan, 84; Louvre, Paris, 26, 85; Freer Gallery of Art, 28; Photo Garo, 29, 72; Landesbibliothek Gotha, 31, 32, 88; Matenadaran, Erevan, 33; Edition du Cercle d'Art, 33; Armenian Patriarchate, Jerusalem, 34, opposite page 64; Studium Biblium Franciscanum, Jerusalem, 47, 81; Metropolitan Museum of Art, N.Y., 48; British Museum, London, 50, 53, 58, 59; Photo Keren-Or, 49, 70; Chuzeville, 64; Photo Hirmer, 67; Bild Archiv Oester, National Bibliothek, 73; Beit el-Din Museum, Lebanon, 84; Photo Skira, opposite page 80; Werner Braun, opposite page 96, opposite page 112; Archives Nationales, Paris, 19; J. Schweig, 21; Cabinet des Medailles, Paris, 45; Israel Air Force, 75, 77; Shraga Kedar, 55; Carta, Jerusalem, maps on pages 44, 66, 134.

Index

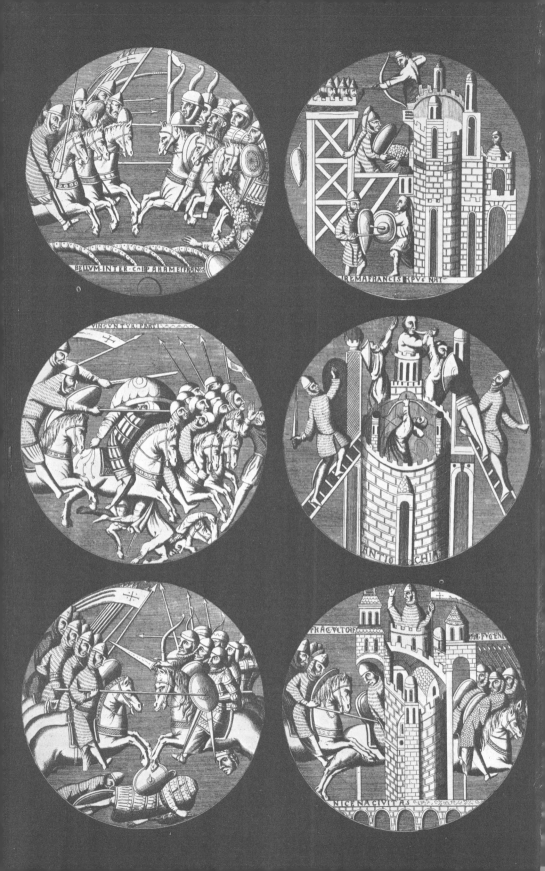